KV-575-208

30150   018923547

FAMILY LAW (SCOTLAND) ACT
1985

AUSTRALIA
LBC Information Services—Sydney

CANADA and USA
Carswell—Toronto

NEW ZEALAND
Brooker's—Auckland

SINGAPORE and MALAYSIA
Sweet & Maxwell Asia
Singapore and Kuala Lumpur

27. Interpretation.
28. Amendments, repeals and savings.
29. Citation, commencement and extent.
     SCHEDULES:
     Schedule 1—Minor and consequential amendments.
     Schedule 2—Repeals.

An Act to make fresh provision in the law of Scotland regarding aliment; regarding financial and other consequences of decrees of divorce and of declarator of nullity of marriage; regarding property rights and legal capacity of married persons; and for connected purposes.

[July 16, 1985]

ABBREVIATIONS

The 1981 Report: *Scottish Law Commission Reports on Aliment and Financial Provision* (Scot. Law Com. No. 67).

The 1984 Report: *Matrimonial Property* (Scot. Law Com. No. 86).

The 1985 Act: Family Law (Scotland) Act 1985.

The 1991 Act: Child Support Act 1991 (as amended by the Child Support Act 1995).

The 1992 Report: *Family Law* (Scot. Law Com. No. 135).

The 1997 Research: Wasoff, F., McGuckin, A. and Edwards, L., *Mutual Consent: Written Agreements in Family Law* (Scottish Office Home Department Central Research Unit, 1997).

The 1999 Act: Welfare Reform and Pensions Act 1999.

The 1999 Bill: Child Support, Pensions and Social Security Bill.

The 1999 Consultation Paper: Scottish Office Home Department, *Improving Scottish Family Law*.

The 1999 White Paper: *A New Contract for Welfare: Children's Rights and Parents' Responsibilities*, Cm. 4349 (1999).

INTRODUCTION AND GENERAL NOTE

The Act constructed a new legal framework for the financial and property aspects of family relationships. In so doing it both reflected and innovated radical changes in family life. It represented a final shift from treating marriage as a relationship of regulated dependency to one of partnership. The Act accommodated the possible permutations of earning and acquisition during a relationship. It set out an even-handed framework for alimentary support. It allowed for a sophisticated "balance sheet" of both financial and non-financial contributions to be drawn up at the end of a marriage and specifically included pension interests in the equation. It introduced a wide range of possible orders.

This potential complexity and flexibility has been achieved at the price of predictability and consistency. The task of tackling the wide range of possible financial arrangements is extremely well suited to mediation, quite appropriate for negotiation but ill served by litigation. In mediation, information is assembled and various options are explored in a co-operative problem-solving way. Negotiation also allows details to be exchanged and a number of possibilities to be investigated. Litigation tends to be more of a collision of aspirations than an attempt at realistic planning. Family actions are usually a jigsaw of competing claims. A crave for one party may make little sense without a complementary crave by the other. The craves may end up creating separate incomplete pictures rather than one whole one. Options hearings appeared to offer a less adversarial and more inquisitorial approach. This could have facilitated creative use of the Act. In practice, options hearings have in most courts become brief formal stages in procedure.

The Divorce (Scotland) Act 1976 contained the previous law of financial provision on divorce. A wide discretion was bestowed upon the courts, although in practice, the options were limited and the outcome fairly predictable. The Scottish Law Commission published a *Report on Aliment and Financial Provision* in November 1981 (Scot. Law Com. No. 67) and a *Report on Matrimonial Property* in June 1984 (Scot. Law Com. No. 86). The Act followed the

FAMILY LAW (SCOTLAND) ACT 1985*

(1985, c. 37)

ARRANGEMENT OF SECTIONS

Aliment

SECT.
1. Obligation of aliment.
2. Actions for aliment.
3. Powers of court in action for aliment.
4. Amount of aliment.
5. Variation or recall of decree of aliment.
6. Interim aliment.
7. Agreements on aliment.

Financial provision on divorce, etc.

8. Orders for financial provision.
9. Principles to be applied.
10. Sharing of value of matrimonial property.
11. Factors to be taken into account.
12. Orders for payment of capital sum or transfer of property.
13. Orders for periodical allowance.
14. Incidental orders.
15. Rights of third parties.
16. Agreements on financial provision.
17. Financial provision on declarator of nullity of marriage.

Supplemental

18. Orders relating to avoidance transactions.
19. Inhibition and arrestment.
20. Provision of details of resources.
21. Award of aliment or custody where divorce or separation refused.
22. Expenses of action.
23. Actions for aliment of small amounts.

Matrimonial property, etc.

24. Marriage not to affect property rights or legal capacity.
25. Presumption of equal shares in household goods.
26. Presumption of equal shares in money and property derived from housekeeping allowance.

Published in 2000 by W. Green & Son Ltd
21 Alva Street
Edinburgh EH2 4PS

Typeset by York House Typographic
Printed and bound in Great Britain by Athenaeum Press Ltd,
Gateshead, Tyne & Wear

No natural forests were destroyed to make this product;
only farmed timber was used and replanted

A CIP catalogue record for this book is available from the
British Library

ISBN 0 414 01374 3

© W. Green and Son Ltd.

All rights reserved. UK statutory material in this publication is
acknowledged as Crown copyright.

No part of this publication may be reproduced or transmitted
in any form or by any means, or stored in any retrieval system
of any nature without prior written permission, except for
permitted fair dealing under the Copyright, Designs and
Patents Act 1988, or in accordance with the terms of a licence
issued by the Copy right Licensing Agency in respect of
photocopying and/or reprographic reproduction. Application
for permission for other use of copyright material including
permission to reproduce extracts in other published works shall
be made to the publishers. Full acknowledgment of author,
publisher and source must be given.

RKS Hall.

FAMILY LAW (SCOTLAND) ACT
1985

Anne Hall Dick

Solicitor
Anne Hall Dick and Co., Solicitors,
Glasgow and Kilmarnock

EDINBURGH UNIVERSITY LIBRARY
WITHDRAWN
EDINBURGH
LAW
&
EUROPA
LIBRARY
UNIVERSITY

W. GREEN/Sweet & Maxwell Ltd
EDINBURGH
2000

recommendations in these Reports. Further changes were proposed in the Scottish Law Commission's *Report on Family Law* (Scot. Law Com. No. 135)—in May 1992 some of these were implemented in the Children (Scotland) Act 1995. A consultation paper—*Improving Scottish Family Law*, was issued by the Scottish Office Home Department in March 1999. It seeks views about various matters including the possibility of implementing more of the proposals from the 1992 Report and of introducing amendments to the 1985 Act. The amendments would deal with issues which have arisen from the application of the Act and are mentioned at the relevant point in the notes.

There has been a significant amount of litigation arising from the Act and an ever-growing number of reported cases. Some of the earlier cases made only tentative use of the Act and did so with little clarity as to the specific elements. The more recent cases disclose a more structured approach although in general, case law has not produced many clear signposts. Great emphasis has been placed on allowing a wide discretion with the result that for any case which appears to settle a particular point there is often another with the opposite outcome.

The majority of couples negotiate rather than litigate about the financial consequences of their separation. Research has been carried out into this process (Wasoff, A., McGuckin, A. and Edwards, L., *Mutual Consent: Written Agreements in Family Law* (Scottish Office Home Department Central Research Unit, 1997).) This suggested that in negotiation rather restricted use was being made of the provisions of the Act. As practitioners have gained more familiarity with the Act negotiated settlements are now taking more of the complex possibilities into account.

ARRANGEMENT OF THE ACT

Aliment
Sections 1–7 regulate the liability for, and mechanics of, financial support between married couples and for children (in some cases up to and including 24 years of age). The Child Support Act 1991 has largely eroded the jurisdiction of the courts in regulating aliment for children who are still at school.

Financial Provision on Divorce
Sections 8–17 set out the framework for financial provision on divorce from the broad principles to the detailed practice. They provide a definition of matrimonial property and a framework for its division on divorce.
Sections 18–23 contain procedural matters including those to safeguard or force disclosure of assets.

Property Rights, Legal Capacity and Presumptions
Sections 24–26 provide that marriage does not affect property rights or legal capacity, but does create presumptions of equal sharing in household goods, and money and property derived from housekeeping allowance.
The Act falls into two main parts—sections 1–7 dealing with alimentary provision and ss.8–23 dealing with financial provision on divorce (or nullity) and ancillary matters. There is a general note for ss.1–7 and one for ss.8–17).

GENERAL NOTE TO SECTIONS 1–7
Sections 1–7 set out for married couples—and for parents and young people—a framework dealing with who is obliged to pay and who is entitled to receive financial support, guidance about the appropriate amount and the mechanics for dealing with claims. The clear picture portrayed has been substantially clouded by the impact of the Child Support Act 1991 which has made its presence felt not only in relation to aliment for children but also for spousal support. Prior to the introduction of the 1991 Act it was open to couples to agree a high level of support for children with no spousal aliment or potential periodical allowance. That approach often suited both parties. Now the Child Support Agency must become involved if the parent with care is on a qualifying benefit (except in very limited circumstances). If a Child Support Agency maintenance assessment is carried out it will render any agreement between the parties

unenforceable (1991 Act, ss.9(1) and 10(2) and the Child Support (Maintenance Arrangements and Jurisdiction) Regulations 1992, reg. 4(1)). It has been recognised that the Agency is currently not providing an adequate system for regulating child support. The 1991 Act introduced a formula for the calculation of child maintenance. It was intended to deliver uniformity in the amount of support provided. After its introduction there was strong criticism leading to substantial amendment of the formula and then to the introduction of some potential discretion in departing from the formula in defined circumstances. Assembling the necessary information and processing it using the formula and potential departures from it has proved time consuming and complicated. Delay and mistakes have occurred. The proposed change in the basis of the calculation is set out in the 1999 Bill. The suggestion is to have a percentage deduction depending on the number of children involved (with some important possible modifications). The figures currently in the Bill are 15 per cent for one child, 20 per cent for two children and 25 per cent for three or more children. This may be significantly lower than the current formula would yield in certain cases, particularly low to mid income non-resident parents with one child. As a result it is possible that spousal support may come into more prominence. For high-earning non-resident parents, the lack of any upper limit in the level of support could lead to much higher payments. The objective is to have the system in place during 2001, and fully functioning by the end of 2003. See the general notes to the Child Support Act at paras A.802 *et seq.*

Interaction with Child Support Act 1991

The 1991 Act does not prevent parents entering into an agreement regulating child support (s.9(2))—although any such agreement cannot exclude the jurisdiction of the Child Support Agency and will be affected should an Agency maintenance assessment be carried out.

Section 8 of the 1991 Act prevents the courts having jurisdiction in relation to making orders for aliment in any case where the Agency has jurisdiction. In most cases where adjudication is required, the Child Support Agency will have exclusive jurisdiction. The Lord Chancellor has made an order in terms of s.5 of the 1991 Act allowing a court to make a maintenance order so long as it incorporates the terms of a written agreement but no order has been made in relation to Scotland by the Lord Advocate.

Exclusion of Child Support Agency jurisdiction

It was originally envisaged that by 1997 the Child Support Agency would have taken over responsibility for regulating maintenance from the courts even if there were existing orders. That timetable proved unrealistic. The courts retain jurisdiction to vary existing orders where the Agency has no jurisdiction (s.8(3A)). The Agency has not yet taken over cases where a written maintenance agreement was made before April 5, 1993 or there is in force a court order for aliment unless the parent with care is receiving a "qualifying benefit" (income support, income based jobseeker's allowance, and formerly family credit and disability working allowance (1991 Act, ss.4(10) and (11), 6(1) and 7(10) and The Child Support (Maintenance Assessment Procedure) Regulations 1992, reg. 34). Receipt of working families' tax credit or of disabled persons' tax credit does not impose a duty to cooperate with the Agency. The Agency *may* have no jurisdiction (other than where a qualifying benefit is in payment to the parent with care) if, even after April 5, 1993, a written agreement is registered in the Books of Council and Session. It has been decided that a registered agreement is a maintenance order in terms of the Child Support (Maintenance Arrangements and Jurisdiction) Regulations 1992, reg. 3 (1)–(5); *Commissioner's Case No. CSCS/5/97* 1999 Fam.L.R. 37). If that interpretation is accepted in relation to s.4(10)(a) of the 1991 Act it would exclude the jurisdiction of the Agency in relation to any non-benefit case where a written agreement dealing with child support is registered in the Books of Council and Session. Subsequent variation would be by agreement or by application to court. The proposed amendment to s.4(10) by the 1999 Bill could restore the Agency's jurisdiction in respect of agreements registered in the future.

The Agency only has jurisdiction in relation to natural parents and cannot make an order against a step parent (1991 Act, s.54).

If any of the parties live outwith the U.K. the Agency does not have jurisdiction (1991 Act, s.44).

The 1991 Act retains the possibility of a court order being made against a parent with care (s.8(10)).

The courts still retain jurisdiction, in terms of the 1991 Act, in relation to provision for school fees and educational and training expenses (s.8(7)) and expenses arising from a child's disability (s.8(8)).

If the "absent parent" is a particularly high earner and an assessment is in force which has included an element calculated under the alternative formula, the courts can make an order for additional payments if satisfied that "the circumstances of the case make it appropriate" (s.8(6)).

If both parents are still in the same household there would be no "absent parent". It would not be treated as "shared care" and so there would be no jurisdiction for the Child Support Agency but the courts would have jurisdiction in terms of s.2(6) of the 1985 Act.

In *Cassidy v. Cassidy*, 1996 Fam.L.B. 21–6 the court allowed variation of a pre-1985 award of aliment lasting until the child was 16 after the young person had reached that age because of the wording of the original award, reserving leave to apply for "any further order that may be required regulating custody and aliment".

In *McGilchrist v. McGilchrist* 1998 S.L.T.(Sh. Ct) 2 there was a detailed explanation of the extension of the transitional provisions and relationship to both court orders and written agreements. It was recognised that the court retained jurisdiction to vary awards of aliment in terms of ss.4(10) and 8(3A) the 1991 Act (as amended) in cases not yet taken over by the Agency.

The restriction on the availability of grants for young people undergoing further education has increased the level of negotiation and litigation in relation to support for students from their parents.

The 1985 Act ended the obligation on children to support their parents. Now the cost of residential care for the elderly is increasingly met from capital resources which otherwise might well have been inherited by the adult children. The public law regime may, in a roundabout way, be creating a partial reversal of the impact of the change in private law.

Aliment

Obligation of aliment

1.—(1) From the commencement of this Act, an obligation of aliment shall be owed by, and only by—
    (a) a husband to his wife;
    (b) a wife to her husband;
    (c) a father or mother to his or her child;
    (d) a person to a child (other than a child who has been boarded out with him by a local or other public authority or a voluntary organisation) who has been accepted by him as a child of his family.

(2) For the purposes of this Act, an obligation of aliment is an obligation to provide such support as is reasonable in the circumstances, having regard to the matters to which a court is required or entitled to have regard under section 4 of this Act in determining the amount of aliment to award in an action for aliment.

(3) Any obligation of aliment arising under a decree or by operation of law and subsisting immediately before the commencement of this Act shall, except insofar as consistent with this section, cease to have effect as from the commencement of this Act.

(4) Nothing in this section shall affect any arrears due under a decree at the date of termination or cessation of an obligation of aliment, nor any rule of law by which a person who is owed an obligation of aliment may claim aliment from the executor of a deceased person or from any person enriched by the succession to the estate of a deceased person.

(5) In subsection (1) above—
"child" means a person—
    (a) under the age of 18 years; or
    (b) over that age and under the age of 25 years who is reasonably and appropriately undergoing instruction at an educational establishment, or training for employment or for a trade, profession or vocation;
"husband" and "wife" include the parties to a valid polygamous marriage.

DEFINITIONS
"action for aliment": ss.2(3) and 27(1).
"aliment": s.27(1).

Family Law Scotland Act 1985

"child": ss.1(5) and 27(1).
"family": s.27(1).
"husband": s.1(5).
"voluntary organisation": s.27(1).
"wife": s.1(5).

GENERAL NOTE

Subs. 1

This details upon whom the obligation of support rests and to whom it is owed. Paragraphs (a) and (b) set out the reciprocal duty between husband and wife (or wives, subs. 5 includes validly constituted polygamous marriages). The obligation continues for as long as the marriage does. It can continue after death. Provision after divorce is a different matter and covered by ss.8(1)(b), 9(1)(c), (d) and (e), and 13(2). The number of wives who work is steadily increasing. At the moment that is reflected more in the relatively low number of claims for aliment by wives than in significant numbers of claims for husbands. Unmarried couples are excluded from the statutory obligation. The 1999 Consultation Paper does not propose extending alimentary provision to include unmarried couples. It is open to them to enter into a contract. This would have to be worded with extreme care since the provisions for potential variation set out in s.7(2) could not be relied on (see *Drummond v. Drummond*, 1996 S.L.T. 386 and 1995 S.C.L.R. 428).

Paragraph (c) imposes an equal obligation on both parents, whether married or unmarried, to provide aliment for their children.

The term "child" is defined in subs. (5) and s.27(1) and includes (in some circumstances) a young person up to, and including, the age of 24. Section 5(1)(a) of the Law Reform (Parent and Child) (Scotland) Act 1986 sets out the presumption that the father of a child born to a married woman is her husband and in s.5(1)(b) that the father, where the parents are not married, is presumed to be the man shown as such in the Register of Births. Adopted children are included in the Adoption (Scotland) Act 1978, ss.38 and 39. The Human Fertilisation and Embryology Act 1990 (ss.27, 28 and 30) regulate more complex parenting.

Accepted as a child of [the] family. This was considered in *Watson v. Watson*, 1994 S.C.L.R. 1097 where it came to light after divorce that a child for whom aliment was being paid was not a child of the marriage. It was considered in those circumstances acceptance could not be imposed retrospectively. The circumstances were unusual but the case underlines the need for conscious acceptance rather than just being under the same roof. Stepfathers are the most likely candidates for liability but the wording could include a grandmother or uncle or aunt (*Inglis v. Inglis and Minuters*, 1987 S.C.L.R. 608). Foster children are excluded.

Subs. (2)

Liability is restricted to what is reasonable as outlined in s.4. Sections 1(2), 4(1) and 3(1)(b) should be read together allowing all the circumstances to be looked at, not restricting aliment to basic necessities (*Winter v. Thornton*, 1993 S.C.L.R. 389).

Subss. (3) and (4)

All other obligations of aliment (excluding arrears due at commencement) are abolished other than the right of a widow or children to claim aliment from the deceased's estate under the common law rule of aliment *jure representationis*. In *Greig v. Greig's Exrs*, 1990 G.W.D. 15–834 ss.1(4), 2 and 4 were taken into account to consider a widow's claim and aliment was awarded for one year.

Subs. (5)

Reasonably and appropriately undergoing instruction at an educational establishment. A claim for aliment for a young person electing to go on to further education could be challenged where the final objective of the education seems obscure but the issue is usually quantum rather than the appropriateness of the instruction.

An expired award of child aliment in favour of the other parent can be taken into account along with other information about needs and resources (*Jowett v. Jowett*, 1990 S.C.L.R. 348). The definition of "educational establishment" was considered in *McBride v. McBride*, 1995 S.C.L.R. 1021.

Training for employment or for a trade, profession or vocation. This could lead to scrutiny of whether a young person is an employee or a trainee. In either case any money paid over to the person for their work may well be very modest and intended to cover expenses such as travel and equipment. Aliment could still be awarded in respect of a young person under 18 who is working but receiving little income (*Wilson v. Wilson* 1987 G.W.D. 4–106).

Actions for aliment

2.—(1) A claim for aliment only (whether or not expenses are also sought) may be made, against any person owing an obligation of aliment, in the Court of Session or the sheriff court.

(2) Unless the court considers it inappropriate in any particular case, a claim for aliment may also be made, against any person owing an obligation of aliment, in proceedings—

    (a) for divorce, separation, declarator of marriage or declarator of nullity of marriage;

    (b) relating to orders for financial provision;

[1] (c) concerning parental responsibilities or parental rights (within the meaning of sections 1(3) and 2(4) respectively of the Children (Scotland) Act 1995) or guardianship in relation to children;

    (d) concerning parentage or legitimacy;

    (e) of any other kind, where the court considers it appropriate to include a claim for aliment.

(3) In this Act "action for aliment" means a claim for aliment in proceedings referred to in subsection (1) or (2) above.

[2] (4) An action for aliment may be brought—

    (a) by a person (including a child) to whom the obligation of aliment is owed;

    (b) by the curator bonis of an incapax;

    (c) on behalf of a child under the age of 18 years, by—

        (i) the parent or guardian of the child;

[1]   (iii) a person with whom the child lives or who is seeking a residence order (within the meaning of section 11(2)(c) of the Children (Scotland) Act 1995) in respect of the child.

(5) A woman (whether married or not) may bring an action for aliment on behalf of her unborn child as if the child had been born, but no such action shall be heard or disposed of prior to the birth of the child.

(6) It shall be competent to bring an action for aliment, notwithstanding that the person for or on behalf of whom aliment is being claimed is living in the same household as the defender.

(7) It shall be a defence to an action for aliment brought by virtue of subsection (6) above that the defender is fulfilling the obligation of aliment, and intends to continue doing so.

(8) It shall be a defence to an action for aliment by or on behalf of a person other than a child under the age of 16 years that the defender is making an offer, which it is reasonable to expect the person concerned to accept, to receive that person into his household and to fulfil the obligation of aliment.

(9) For the purposes of subsection (8) above, in considering whether it is reasonable to expect a person to accept an offer, the court shall have regard among other things to any conduct, decree or other circumstances which appear to the court to be relevant: but the fact that a husband and wife have agreed to live apart shall not of itself be regarded as making it unreasonable to expect a person to accept such an offer.

(10) A person bringing an action for aliment under subsection (4)(c) above may give a good receipt for aliment paid under the decree in the action.

NOTES

    1. Substituted by the Children (Scotland) Act 1995 (c. 36), Sched. 4, para. 36.

    2. As amended by the Age of Legal Capacity (Scotland) Act 1991 (c. 50), Sched. 1, para. 40 and Sched. 2.

DEFINITIONS

    "action": s.27(1).

"action for aliment": ss.2(3) and 27(1).
"aliment": s.27(1).
"court": s.27(1).
"decree": s.27(1).
"parental responsibilities": s.1(3) of the Children (Scotland) Act 1995.
"parental rights": s.2(4) of the Children (Scotland) Act 1995.
"residence order": s.11(2)(c) of the Children (Scotland) Act 1995.
"obligation of aliment": s.27(1).
"child": s.27(1).

GENERAL NOTE

Subs. (2)
It can be helpful to have all the outstanding issues sorted out in one action. The Child Support Act does restrict that possibility.

Subs. (4)
Paragraphs (a) and (c) present a choice. Either child or parent can take proceedings if a child is under 18. In practice it is usual for the parent to make a claim for the child while at school but for the obligation to be constituted between parent and child once the child goes on to further education.

Subs. (6)
It can be necessary to negotiate short-term arrangements in the period before actual separation. Where a couple (or either party to the couple) believe that a separation is inevitable but housing is a real issue and they remain under the same roof the financial relationship can be very fragile. In those circumstances divorce proceedings might well be raised while the parties still live together. The court could regulate both spousal and child aliment. (See General Note to ss.1–7.)

Subs. (8)
This defence is not available if aliment is being claimed by or on behalf of a child under 16. Where residence is an issue that would have to be dealt with openly, not obliquely. Child aliment will normally be dealt with by the CSA in any event.
The defence could arise if a young person wished to pursue further education and the liable parent believed this could be achieved using that parent's home as a base. If the young person did not agree and adjudication were required, the factors to be taken into account would include the availability of suitable courses and the behaviour of the parties—in addition to the financial aspects.

Subs. (9)
An agreement to live apart may not be sufficient to make it unreasonable to accept an offer. Any lower earning spouse contemplating leaving home where the relationship has become becalmed rather than shipwrecked should have a binding contract for aliment in place! Behaviour which would not provide grounds for divorce may be enough to justify living apart.

Powers of court in action for aliment

3.—(1) The court may, if it thinks fit, grant decree in an action for aliment, and in granting such decree shall have power—
  (a) to order the making of periodical payments, whether for a definite or an indefinite period or until the happening of a specified event;
  (b) to order the making of alimentary payments of an occasional or special nature, including payments in respect of inlying, funeral or educational expenses;
  (c) to backdate an award of aliment under this Act—
    (i) to the date of the bringing of the action or to such later date as the court thinks fit; or
    (ii) on special cause shown, to a date prior to the bringing of the action;
  (d) to award less than the amount claimed even if the claim is undisputed.

(2) Nothing in subsection (1) above shall empower the court to substitute a lump sum for a periodical payment.

DEFINITIONS
"action": s.27(1).
"action for aliment": ss.2(3) and 27(1).
"aliment": s.27(1).
"the court": s.27(1).
"decree": s.27(1).

GENERAL NOTE

Subs. (1)

Para. (a)
Periodical payments. This covers the most common situation of imposing weekly or monthly payments. The importance of appropriate wording was highlighted in *Drummond v. Drummond*, 1996 S.L.T. 386. A separation agreement used the term "aliment" for money payable after divorce. There was no provision in the agreement for variation. An attempt to vary the agreement after the parties were divorced using s.7(2) failed since aliment was not an obligation owed after divorce and s.16(1)(a) was not available because there was no provision for variation by the court and it was too late to involve s.16(1)(b). Financial provision for a spouse after divorce should be described as "periodical allowance" and the possibility of setting it aside or varying it in terms of s.16(1)(a) specified.

Para. (b)
Occasional or special nature. It is competent to make a general order in respect of educational expenses under this subsection rather than fixing a specific amount (*Macdonald v. Macdonald*, 1993 S.C.L.R. 132). Factors to be considered include the liable parent's original attitude to taking on the commitment (see *Macdonald*) but also capacity to pay (*McGeoch v. McGeoch*, 1996 Fam.L.B. 23–8).

Para. (c)
The courts are loath to make an order for backdating. This could be exploited by a reluctant payer. *Buchan v. Buchan*, 1993 S.C.L.R. 158 underlined that backdating prior to the date of proceedings will be done in exceptional circumstances only. In that case negotiations had been taking place but were unsuccessful. The fact that support, which had been available during 29 years of marriage, had stopped did not in itself amount to special circumstances where the wife had income of her own to meet her immediate needs. Special cause means something more than the usual refusal to pay (*Adamson v. Adamson*, 1994 Fam.L.B. 9–7). A failure to obtemper a court order or seek to have it varied did not amount to special circumstances (*Hannah v. Hannah*, 1988 S.L.T. 82). Backdating has been granted where factors other than simple delay in negotiations have been present. The existence of a prior decree for child aliment coupled with consistent efforts to press for a continuation of support by the young person in her own right was accepted as special cause to allow backdating to the date of the cessation of the prior decree (*Mitchell v. Mitchell*, 1992 S.C.L.R. 553).
Where a husband did pay aliment until he became unemployed, promptly intimated his inability to pay to his former wife and she appeared initially to accept the situation special circumstances were accepted (*Abrahams v. Abrahams*, 1989 S.L.T.(Sh. Ct) 11).
A decision by the DHSS that a father need not pay them a contribution towards a child's aliment was accepted as grounds to backdate a downwards variation of aliment to the date of that decision, though not to cover an earlier period of non-payment (*Dalgleish v. Robinson*, 1991 S.C.L.R. 892).
It is clear that backdating should never be relied on and that a tight timetable for negotiations is needed. When acting for the payer it is crucial to provide advice at the time the obligation is constituted about the need to intimate promptly any change of circumstances and to have that followed up more formally without delay. (If the obligation is set out in a separation agreement rather than a court order, a clause suspending payment during a period of unemployment of which notice and evidence is provided is particularly necessary since backdating and interim variation is not possible in relation to variation of agreements rather than court orders in terms of s.7.)

Para. (d)

Full information should always be provided to justify a request for aliment and support the amount requested. Inflated figures intended to allow room for manoeuvre may dent credibility even if the action is not opposed!

Subs. (2)

This prevents capitalisation of child support and of spousal support before divorce.

Amount of aliment

4.—(1) In determining the amount of aliment to award in an action for aliment, the court shall, subject to subsection (3) below, have regard—

(a) to the needs and resources of the parties;

(b) to the earning capacities of the parties;

(c) generally to all the circumstances of the case.

(2) Where two or more parties owe an obligation of aliment to another person, there shall be no order of liability, but the court, in deciding how much, if any, aliment to award against any of those persons, shall have regard, among the other circumstances of the case, to the obligation of aliment owed by any other person.

(3) In having regard under subsection (1)(c) above generally to all the circumstances of the case, the court—

(a) may, if it thinks fit, take account of any support, financial or otherwise, given by the defender to any person whom he maintains as a dependant in his household, whether or not the defender owes an obligation of aliment to that person; and

(b) shall not take account of any conduct of a party unless it would be manifestly inequitable to leave it out of account.

[1] (4) Where a court makes an award of aliment in an action brought by or on behalf of a child under the age of 16 years, it may include in that award such provision as it considers to be in all the circumstances reasonable in respect of the expenses incurred wholly or partly by the person having care of the child for the purpose of caring for the child.

NOTE

1. Added by the Child Support Act 1991 (c. 48), Sched. 5, para. 5.

DEFINITIONS

"action for aliment": ss.2(3) and 27(1).

"aliment": s.27(1).

"child": s.27(1).

"the court": s.27(1).

"needs": s.27(1).

"obligation of aliment": ss.1(2) and 27(1).

"resources": s.27(1).

GENERAL NOTE

Subsection 1 provides an admirably broad starting point encouraging common sense and flexibility. Unfortunately, even in quite amicable negotiations the production of information about income and outgoings usually discloses that the needs of each household exceed available income. Apportioning liability for debt is not uncommon. In negotiations it can be helpful to start from comparing basic outlays in connection with housing, food and utilities then considering existing contractual debt before widening out to looking at other expenditure.

Concentration on core costs to start with can do something to avoid unhelpful debate over what is necessary expenditure.

It is still open to couples to negotiate both spousal and child support and set this down in an enforceable contract. In view of the length of time it can take for a Child Support Agency assessment to be carried out this is often the preferred course. It also allows more flexibility than the Child Support Agency formula provides. It must always be borne in mind that if an Agency assessment is carried out subsequently any provision for child aliment in a contract between them will be unenforceable during the currency of the assessment. (See General Note.)

(a) *Needs and resources.*

   (i) *Needs.* A parent could not be allowed to place any items of non-essential expenditure before the reasonable aliment of his child (*Sutherland v. Sutherland*, 1991 G.W.D. 38–2299). Equally, capacity to pay is an essential consideration (*McGeoch v. McGeoch*, 1996 Fam.L.B. 23–8 and 1996 G.W.D. 29–1751).

   (ii) *Resources.* Income from employment, self employment and investments will be taken into account as will state benefits—such as child benefit—which are not means tested. Capital is not usually taken into account except in so far as it generates income (which is also the approach taken by the Child Support Agency). Usually entitlement to a state benefit such as income support should not be taken into account (*McCarrol v. McCarrol*, 1966 S.L.T.(Sh. Ct) 45) (but see *Smith v. Smith*, 1988 S.L.T. 840). If the potential payer of aliment is living with a new partner who is working, then the new partner's income is only taken into account to reflect the fact that some of the joint household costs of the new couple will be shared (*Munro v. Munro*, 1986 S.L.T. 72 and *Frith v. Frith*, 1990 G.W.D. 5–266). In *Semple v. Semple*, 1995 S.C.L.R. 569 the benefit of a company car and payment of pension contributions were considered resources to be taken into account in considering an appropriate level of aliment. They were not, however, to be simply added in to the calculation as if actual income but to be reflected in the overall picture.

   (iii) *Needs* and *resources.* Both are defined in s.27 as "present and foreseeable"; any imminent change should be taken into account.

(b) *Earning capacities.* There is similar provision in the formula for maintenance assessments under the Child Support Act although less flexibility in how it can be applied. This subsection could allow a spouse who chooses not to work overtime to be found liable to pay a higher level of support than his basic pay would justify. Earning capacity has been taken into account in making educational orders (*Macdonald v. Macdonald*, 1993 S.C.L.R. 132). It is less likely to impose on the parent caring for children the duty to work outside the home. It could mean a student is expected to work part-time while undergoing further education.

(c) *All the circumstances of the case.* This does emphasise how each case must be taken on its own merits. Tax relief on payments of aliment has been gradually eroded and the modest allowance available will be largely abolished with effect from April 2000. The equivalent of net income is usually the basis of the calculations an approach reinforced by the abolition of tax relief on the payments.

Subs. (2)

Apportioning liability can arise between parents (*Scully v. Scully*, 1989 S.C.L.R. 757) or where adults have accepted a child as a member of their family and aliment is being requested from a natural parent (*Inglis v. Inglis and Minuters*, 1987 S.C.L.R. 608).

Subs. (3)

Para. (a)

Dependants. This allows consideration of the needs of a new partner and his or her children even where no legal obligation of aliment exists.

Para. (b)

Conduct. The Act does allow the possibility of taking conduct into account but only if "it would be manifestly inequitable to leave it out of account". There is similar provision in respect of financial support after divorce in s.11(7)(b). In *Macdonald v. Macdonald*, 1993 S.C.L.R. 132 the father's insistence on private education was taken into account. Subsequent cohabitation by the claimant may not end entitlement to spousal aliment (*Kavanagh v. Kavanagh*, 1989 S.L.T. 134 which distinguished *Brunton v. Brunton*, 1986 S.L.T. 49) although it is a very important factor. In practice it is usually accepted as inequitable and inappropriate for spousal aliment to be payable to a spouse who is cohabiting with a new partner and a number of separation agreements include that restriction. Expense occasioned by child care can be included in child aliment in terms of subs. (4).

Subs. (4)

This addition brought court-based aliment for a child in line with a maintenance assessment from the Child Support Agency to the extent of allowing an element for the carer in the calculation. The agency formula has since been amended to modify, in some cases, that element depending on the age of the child or children involved.

Variation or recall of decree of aliment

5.—(1) A decree granted in an action for aliment brought before or after the commencement of this Act may, on an application by or on behalf of either party to the action, be varied or recalled by an order of the court if since the date of the decree there has been a material change of circumstances.

[1] (1A) Without prejudice to the generality of subsection (1) above, the making of a maintenance assessment with respect to a child for whom the decree of aliment was granted is a material change of circumstances for the purposes of that subsection.

(2) The provisions of this Act shall apply to applications and orders under subsection (1) above as they apply to actions for aliment and decrees in such actions, subject to any necessary modifications.

(3) On an application under subsection (1) above, the court may, pending determination of the application, make such interim order as it thinks fit.

(4) Where the court backdates an order under subsection (1) above, the court may order any sums paid under the decree to be repaid.

NOTE
1. Inserted by S.I. 1993 No. 660.

DEFINITIONS
"action for aliment": ss.2(3) and 27(1).
"aliment": s.27(1).
"child": s.27(1).
"the court": s.27(1).
"decree": s.27(1).
"maintenance assessment": s.27(1) and s.54 of the Child Support Act 1991.

GENERAL NOTE
The interaction of subss. (1), (2) and (3) is particularly important in allowing interim variation and backdating where aliment is constituted in a court order as those possibilities are not extended by s.7 dealing with variation of agreements. Care should be taken however if a decree supersedes an agreement that all the loose ends are tied up (*Mills v. Mills*, 1990 S.C.L.R. 213).

Material change of circumstances. There has been some divergence as to what constitutes a material change. In *Kirkpatrick v. Kirkpatrick*, 1993 S.C.L.R. 175 inflation and general increases in childcare costs were not accepted as sufficient to constitute material change of circumstances. It was recommended that the original decision should be taken as the base line. In *Skinner v. Skinner*, 1996 S.C.L.R. 334 it was accepted that if the costs of maintaining a child increased over the years this is a change of circumstances and that aspect of *Kirkpatrick* was not followed. The general approach of taking the original award as the base-line was not challenged (see *Macpherson v. Macpherson*, 1989 S.L.T. 231, which also takes that approach in relation to periodical allowance). If spousal aliment has been ordered on an interim basis at a time when no CSA maintenance assessment has been made, the amount of spousal aliment will not automatically be reduced by the amount of any subsequent maintenance assessment. A general reassessment will be carried out (*Stokes v. Stokes*, 1999 S.C.L.R. 327).

Proving a material change of circumstances may not justify a downward variation. In *Joshi v. Joshi*, 1998 G.W.D. 8–357 variation to nil was refused after the father's remarriage and birth of another child as it was considered he could still afford the amount awarded in 1992. Aliment was considered a priority over Sky T.V.

Subsection 2 extends the wider provisions in relation to aliment to actions for variation or recall including the possibility of backdating. This happened in *Milne v. Milne*, 1992 S.C.L.R. 600, which allowed a backdated downwards variation where it came to light during divorce proceedings that the wife had been working while receiving aliment. In *McColl v. McColl*, 1993 S.L.T. 617 the First Division noted that there was no provision for backdating variation of interim aliment. There was a limit as to what could be achieved by backdating a permanent award, which could only help if the interim award turned out to be lower than the permanent one.

Non-disclosure of material facts. A lack of frankness is frowned on by the Bench. In *Spowart v. McKenzie*, 1996 Fam.L.B. 23–8 an ex-wife was granted an upward variation of her children's aliment. The ex-husband appealed. Before the appeal was dealt with, the wife discovered that the ex-husband had received a substantial inheritance, which had not been taken into account. Since it was the material fact and the ex-husband had known about it and should have disclosed it, the impact of the legacy was taken into account in the appeal.

Interim aliment

6.—(1) A claim for interim aliment shall be competent—

(a) in an action for aliment, by the party who claims aliment against the other party;

(b) in an action for divorce, separation, declarator of marriage or declarator of nullity of marriage, by either party against the other party,

on behalf of the claimant and any person on whose behalf he is entitled to act under section 2(4) of this Act.

(2) Where a claim under subsection (1) above has been made, then, whether or not the claim is disputed, the court may award by way of interim aliment the sum claimed or any lesser sum or may refuse to make such an award.

(3) An award under subsection (2) above shall consist of an award of periodical payments payable only until the date of the disposal of the action in which the award was made or such earlier date as the court may specify.

(4) An award under subsection (2) above may be varied or recalled by an order of the court; and the provisions of this section shall apply to an award so varied and the claim therefor as they applied to the original award and the claim therefor.

DEFINITIONS

"action for aliment": ss.2(3) and 27(1).
"aliment": s.27(1).
"the court": s.27(1).

GENERAL NOTE

This allows short-term arrangements to be made wherever longer-term financial support is requested.

Subs. (2)

This emphasises the need for full information to support any such claim and the importance of requesting a reasonable figure based on that information to retain credibility with the court.

Subs. (4)

This makes provision for variation of interim aliment.

Awards in the short-term may be made without full information being available and without all the aspects relevant in the long-term being taken into account. They may, however, have a strong influence on the longer-term arrangements. It is very important to be fully prepared especially in view of the lack of adjustment possible should an interim award turn out to have been too high (*McColl v. McColl*, 1993 S.L.T. 617). The interaction of spousal aliment and means tested benefits can make a request for interim aliment of little practical benefit. An award of interim aliment can affect the possibility of including an element of capitalised periodical allowance in an overall negotiated settlement. The impact on any available means tested benefits would have to be taken into account.

Bisset v. Bisset, 1993 S.C.L.R. 284. There did not need to have been a change of circumstances to justify variation in terms of s.6(4)—simply sufficient reason.

Stokes v. Stokes, 1999 S.C.L.R. 327. The sheriff principal upheld a decision declining to reduce spousal aliment payable *ad interim* by exactly the amount of a subsequent maintenance assessment and instead carrying out a general reassessment.

B v. B, 1999 Fam. L.R. 74. In awarding interim spousal aliment, Lord Marnoch took into account financial resources available to the husband, not just the salary drawn from the business, and included a figure for outgoings being paid by the husband for the wife.

Agreements on aliment

7.—(1) Any provision in an agreement which purports to exclude future liability for aliment or to restrict any right to bring an action for aliment shall have no effect unless the provision was fair and reasonable in all the circumstances of the agreement at the time it was entered into.

(2) Where a person who owes an obligation of aliment to another person has entered into an agreement to pay aliment to or for the benefit of the other person, on a material change of circumstances application may be made to the court by or on behalf of either person for variation of the amount payable under the agreement or for termination of the agreement.

[1] (2A) Without prejudice to the generality of subsection (2) above, the making of a maintenance assessment with respect to a child to whom or for whose benefit aliment is payable under such an agreement is a material change of circumstances for the purposes of that subsection.

(3) Subsections (8) and (9) of section 2 of this Act (which afford a defence to an action for aliment in certain circumstances) shall apply to an action to enforce such an agreement as is referred to in subsection (2) above as they apply to an action for aliment.

(4) In subsection (2) above "the court" means the court which would have jurisdiction and competence to entertain an action for aliment between the parties to the agreement to which the application under that subsection relates.

(5) In this section "agreement" means an agreement entered into before or after the commencement of this Act and includes a unilateral voluntary obligation.

NOTE
    1. Inserted by S.I. 1993 No. 660.

DEFINITIONS
    "action for aliment": ss.2(3) and 27(1).
    "aliment": s.27(1).
    "agreement": s.7(5).
    "child": s.27(1).
    "the court": ss.7(4) and 27(1).
    "maintenance assessment": s.27(1).
    "obligation of aliment": ss.1(2) and 27(1).

GENERAL NOTE

Subs. (2)
    A point to watch is to avoid protracted negotiations attempting to vary aliment due in terms of an agreement followed by litigation as there is no procedure for varying aliment on an interim basis, nor for backdating (*Woolley v. Strachan*, 1997 S.L.T.(Sh. Ct) 88).
    Variation of agreement should proceed by summary application (*Young v. Young*, 1995 G.W.D. 32–1634 and *Woolley v. Strachan*, 1997 S.L.T.(Sh. Ct) 88).
    See note to s.5(1) re *material change of circumstances*.

Financial provision on divorce, etc.

GENERAL NOTE TO SECTIONS 8–17
    Financial provision in the Act was described by Lord President Hope in *Little v. Little*, 1990 S.L.T. 785 at 787 as setting out "in considerable and almost clinical detail the nature of the property with respect of which orders may be made, the principles which are to be applied and the factors which are to be taken into account. No stone seems to have been left unturned in this analysis. The court is taken step by step through a complicated check list of provisions to which it must have regard, so that no point which might conceivably be relevant is at risk of being forgotten as it proceeds through the exercise to the result ... But despite all the detail much is

14

still left to the discretion of the court. This is clear from an examination of s.8(2), which provides that the court shall make such order, if any, as is justified by the principles set out in s.9 and reasonable having regard to the resources of the parties. The concept of sharing the net value of the matrimonial property fairly, the flexibility which is given by the expression "special circumstances" in s.10(6) and the repeated references in s.11 to all the other circumstances of the case serve to emphasise that, despite the detail, the matter is essentially one of discretion, aimed at achieving a fair and practicable result in accordance with common sense. It remains as important as it has always been that the details should be left in the hands of the court of first instance and not opened up for re-consideration on appeal."

From a review of decided cases it could be concluded that neither clinical detail nor common sense have been particularly prevalent. Prior to the Act the courts' discretion was wide, but the options narrow. With the implementation of Act the courts' discretion was narrowed, but their options considerably widened. It has taken some time for Bench and Bar to make the necessary adjustment.

Full information and explanation is necessary in the pleadings and judgments to make sense and use of the provisions of the Act.

Section 8 (as expanded by s.14) provides the range of possible orders and s.9(1)(a)–(e) sets out the broad principles used to decide which of those, if any, should be granted. The starting point in s.9(1)(a) is that the net value of the matrimonial property at the relevant date should be shared fairly, which in terms of s.10(1) is to be taken to be equally or in such other proportions as are justified by special circumstances. Examples of special circumstances are given in s.10(6). Subsections (2)–(5) of s.10 set out how to define and calculate the value of the net matrimonial property. Section 11 sets out the factors to be taken into account in applying the principles set out in s.9(1)(b)–(e) specifically. Section 11(7)(a) allows conduct to be taken into account for any of the s.9 principles if it has adversely affected the relevant financial resources and s.11(7)(b) if it would be manifestly inequitable to leave it out of account in relation to s.9(d) and (e).

The potential delay between the relevant date and the making of an order under the Act can complicate matters. See the note to s.8(1)(aa).

Orders for periodical allowance under s.8(2) can only be made if justified under Subss (1)(c), (d) or (e) of s.9. No such order can be made unless payment of a capital sum or transfer of property is ruled out. This encourages the possibility of a "clean break" although s.12(3) allows a payment of capital under s.8(2) to be paid by instalments. An order for periodical allowance can potentially be varied in terms of s.13(4) on a material change of circumstances that could include reducing or cancelling the liability. An order for capital payable by instalments can also be varied in terms of s.12(4) but only as regards the date or method of payment or date of transfer. Instalments of capital are thus likely to be more attractive to the recipient and periodical allowance to the payer. The Act is, in retrospect, an imaginative combination of defined external boundaries and internal flexibility. It fixes the time-frame for, and definition of, matrimonial property in order to focus on what is generated within the marriage from the efforts of the couple. It allows financial and non-financial contributions to be taken into account. It is perhaps not surprising that it has taken some time for the full possibilities of the Act to be explored and anomalies to be identified, some of which are now being addressed in the 1999 Consultation Paper. The complex interplay of the various principles is proving difficult to exploit in litigation and does give rise to some problems in advising clients and negotiations between them. Because of the emphasis on discretion very few guiding principles have emerged. *Little v. Little*, 1990 S.L.T. 785 and 1991 S.C.L.R. 47, in addition to affirming the importance of judicial discretion, endorsed the possibility of excluding certain items of property from the fund available for division under s.9(1)(a) (see the reservations expressed by Professor Thomson in his commentary on p. 59 of the S.C.L.R. report).

Jacques v. Jacques, 1997 S.L.T. 459 established that the existence alone of special circumstances in terms of s.10(6) did not in itself require a departure from equal sharing in respect of s.9(1)(a) emphasising that any departure also had to be justified. In one of the few appeals which did impose boundaries, *Wallis v. Wallis*, 1993 S.L.T. 1348 it was decided that it was not competent to take account of the increase in value of the matrimonial property between the relevant date and date of divorce when giving effect to s.9(1)(a) even when a transfer of the property was to be ordered with the consequence that the transferee would receive the "windfall" of the increase. One of the proposals in the 1999 Consultation Paper is to allow the value at date of the order to be taken into account in such circumstances. Some decisions appear so nearly "winner take all" as to risk an increase in the likelihood of speculative litigation and could thwart efforts to promote win/win negotiations. *Cunniff v. Cunniff (No. 2)*, 1999 Fam.L.R. 46 upheld a division of property so unequal as to exceed the available property and leave the husband with only debt. Professor Thomson, Glasgow University, has been energetic in urging that more extensive use should be made of the various s.9(1) principles, especially s.9(1)(b) (advantage/disadvantage) and s.14(2)(j) allowing for interest to be payable from earlier than the date of decree. In view of the reluctance of the appeal courts to interfere with decisions at first instance it is extremely important to ensure that any relevant provision is cogently pled and argued.

Orders for financial provision

8.—(1) In an action for divorce, either party to the marriage may apply to the court for one or more of the following orders—

[1] (a) an order for the payment of a capital sum to him by the other party to the marriage;

[2] (aa) an order for the transfer of property to him by the other party to the marriage;

    (b) an order for the making of a periodical allowance to him by the other party to the marriage;

[3] (ba) an order under section 12(A)(2) or (3) of this Act;

    (c) an incidental order within the meaning of section 14(2) of this Act.

(2) Subject to sections 12 to 15 of this Act, where an application has been made under subsection (1) above, the court shall make such order, if any, as is—

    (a) justified by the principles set out in section 9 of this Act; and

    (b) reasonable having regard to the resources of the parties.

(3) An order under subsection (2) above is in this Act referred to as an "order for financial provision".

NOTES
1. As amended by the Law Reform (Miscellaneous Provisions) (Scotland) Act 1990 (c. 40), Sched. 8, para. 34 and Sched. 9.
2. Inserted by the Law Reform (Miscellaneous Provisions) (Scotland) Act 1990 (c. 40), Sched. 8, para. 34.
3. Inserted by the Pensions Act 1995 (c. 26), s.167(1). Section 167(4) of the Pensions Act 1995 provides that "nothing in the provisions mentioned in section 166(5) [of the 1995 Act] applies to a court exercising its powers under section 8(orders for financial provision on divorce, etc.) or 12A (orders for payment of capital sum: pensions lump sums) of the 1985 Act in respect of any benefits under a pension scheme which fall within subsection (5)(b) of section 10 of that Act ("pension scheme" having the meaning given in subsection (10) of that section)."

DEFINITIONS
"action": s.27(1).
"action for divorce": s.17(1).
"the court": s.27(1).
"party to the marriage": s.27(1).
"property": s.27(1).
"resources": s.27(1).

GENERAL NOTE
This section sets out specifically and by incorporation the range of orders that can be made in an action before, on or soon after, the granting of decree of divorce or nullity. Orders in relation to pension interests are to be found in s.12A. Section 14(2)(a) allows the making of an order for the sale of property and s.14(2)(k) gives the general power to make "any ancillary order which is expedient to give effect to the principles set out in section 9 of this Act or to any order made under section 8(2) of this Act".

Subs. (1)

Paras (a) and (aa)
After some early doubt (when the original provision was worded as a capital sum *or* transfer of property) as to whether it was intended to mean "or" or "and/or" the provision was re-worded in its present form to make it quite clear that, if justified by the s.9 principles and reasonable, both a payment of capital and a property transfer order could be made. That was

one aspect the decision in *Little v. Little*, 1990 S.L.T. 230 (a decision upheld by the First Division on appeal, 1990 S.L.T. 785), approved in *Walker v. Walker*, 1991 S.L.T. 157. In the latter case the need for an adequate description of the subjects was emphasised.

Increases in the value of matrimonial property between the relevant date and the date of an order can lead to a collision between the intention of the Act and the common law rules. In *Wallis v. Wallis*, 1993 S.L.T. 1348 the House of Lords upheld an Inner House decision that, where an order for transfer of title was made to give effect to s.9(1)(a), the counterbalancing payment should be based on the value of the property at the relevant date, rather than divorce. By that later time the property had increased in value by 24,000. This case was distinguished in *Lewis v. Lewis*, 1993 S.C.L.R. 32 where, as in some earlier cases, a jointly owned house was excluded from s.9(1)(a) allowing the proceeds to be divided at sale rather than separation. One of the options for reform in the 1999 Consultation Paper is to place a value on any property to be transferred at the date of transfer, rather than the relevant date. The Consultation Paper emphasises that there is no proposal to change the s.9(1)(a) principle which would still apply to the relevant date.

Para. (aa)

If an order for *transfer* is craved it is usually necessary to provide evidence that any heritable creditor will consent in addition to intimating the crave (s.15(1) and (2)). In *MacNaught v. MacNaught*, 1997 S.L.T.(Sh. Ct) 60 the importance of evidence of consent was underlined. It is also important to show the feasibility of the transfer. An order for transfer to a wife was refused in *Shipton v. Shipton*, 1992 S.C.L.R. 23 because it was clear that she could not have coped with the outlay involved.

Subs. 2

Orders must be *both* justified by s.9 principles *and* reasonable.

Macdonald v. Macdonald, 1993 S.C.L.R. 132. A property transfer order was refused as inappropriate as it would have deprived the husband of his only capital asset (but note the decision of *Cunniff v. Cunniff (No. 2)*, 1999 Fam.L.R. 46 where such an outcome was upheld on appeal).

McConnell v. McConnell (No. 2), 1997 Fam.L.R. 108. It was considered reasonable to allow the pursuer periodical allowance for a period of six months to enable her to adjust.

Rodgers v. Rodgers (No. 2), 1994 G.W.D. 31–1869. The only substantial item of matrimonial property was the wife's pension interests. She was using her pension and invalidity benefit to pay back a secured loan. The husband was not awarded a capital sum, as the wife had no other resources.

Fraser v. Fraser, 1995 G.W.D. 14–800. This underlined the need to lead evidence about any resources that a party wishes to have taken into account. If non-matrimonial resources are being looked to as a way of establishing the reasonableness of a full share of matrimonial property being paid this has to be covered in averment and proof. In that case it was not established that the husband had a share in a new home from which a capital payment could be made.

Resources. These are defined in s.27 as "present and foreseeable resources". Where a substantial net matrimonial property had dwindled because of unforeseen difficulties by the date of divorce the award was based on the modest remaining asset (*Shand v. Shand*, 1994 S.L.T. 387). In *Welsh v. Welsh*, 1994 S.L.T. 828 it was observed that the purpose of s.8(2)(b) was to "protect a party who might require to pay a capital sum which he or she could not afford, assuming an equal division as a result of a diminution of the value of items of matrimonial property between the relevant date and the date of the divorce" (p. 835L).

Principles to be applied

9.—(1) The principles which the court shall apply in deciding what order for financial provision, if any, to make are that—

(a) the net value of the matrimonial property should be shared fairly between the parties to the marriage;

(b) fair account should be taken of any economic advantage derived by either party from contributions by the other, and of any economic disadvantage suffered by either party in the interests of the other party or of the family;

(c) any economic burden of caring, after divorce, for a child of the marriage under the age of 16 years should be shared fairly between the parties;

(d) a party who has been dependent to a substantial degree on the financial support of the other party should be awarded such financial provision as is reasonable to enable him to adjust, over a period of not more than three years from the date of the decree of divorce, to the loss of that support on divorce;

(e) a party who at the time of the divorce seems likely to suffer serious financial hardship as a result of the divorce should be awarded such financial provision as is reasonable to relieve him of hardship over a reasonable period.

(2) In subsection (1)(b) above and section 11(2) of this Act—

"economic advantage" means advantage gained whether before or during the marriage and includes gains in capital, in income and in earning capacity, and "economic disadvantage" shall be construed accordingly;

"contributions" means contributions made whether before or during the marriage; and includes indirect and non-financial contributions and, in particular, any such contribution made by looking after the family home or caring for the family.

DEFINITIONS

"child of the marriage": s.27(1).
"the court": s.27(1).
"divorce": s.17(2).
"marriage": s.27(1).
"matrimonial property": s.10(4).
"order for financial provision": s.8(3).
"party to the marriage": s.27(1).

GENERAL NOTE

This section is the heart of financial provision on divorce (or nullity). Any order made must be justified by one of the five principles and also be reasonable having regard to the resources of the parties (s.8(2)(b)). The factors to be taken into account in applying the principles are set out in s.11.

In *Cunniff v. Cunniff (No. 2)*, 1999 Fam.L.R. 46 Lord McCluskey observed that "it is the duty of the court to apply [s.9(1)](a) and also to apply whichever of the other specified principles which are relevant in the light of the facts of the case as established to the satisfaction of the court".

It can be daunting to assess what particular "pik-n-mix" of principles, factors and orders are appropriate in any particular case. A schedule of assets and liabilities is the appropriate starting point to provide a "snapshot" of the net matrimonial property at the relevant date and a schedule of income and expenditure will complete the picture. It is unlikely automatically to deliver the answer to the question of what is appropriate financial provision. The interweaving of provisions does not lend itself to a formulaic approach. The difficulties in applying a formula have, in any.event, been amply demonstrated by the child support legislation. The emphasis on discretion in *Little v. Little* reinforced the importance of principle rather than precedent. Lord McCluskey's observation emphasises the importance of applying s.9(1)(a). That requires the net value of the matrimonial property to be calculated. Then the possibility of "special circumstances" and potential application of the principles in s.9(1)(b) can be considered. The following approach might be of assistance in weighing things up. Consider whether there is any clear indication that the consequence of the marriage has been either to help or hinder either of the parties' career. Has it resulted in one having a career interrupted for child care? If so, what employment had been followed originally? What income did it generate? Was the standard of living during the marriage as good or better than that income could have supported? If so, the career disadvantage may well have been balanced out to an extent but has the interruption of career damaged promotion or pension prospects? If so, how far does the sharing of matrimonial and property generated by the other spouse balance that? Has non-matrimonial property of any sort (including business interests) belonging to one spouse improved in value through the direct or indirect efforts of the other? For "special circumstances" consider whether any matrimonial property has been adversely affected in value by the actions of one spouse. Did either or both bring assets into the marriage or come by way of a gift or inheritance now invested in matrimonial property? How important is that particular family home for the children or any business use? Is a significant amount of the net matrimonial property tied up in a business? Is there any other unusual feature? Remember that in considering the first two principles the focus is on the economic fortunes of the couple in the past (and up to the relevant date so far as "fair sharing" is concerned). Behaviour is relevant only if it has had financial consequences.

Then look to the future. Consider s.9(1)(c) if there are children. Does the likely division of capital allow for adequate housing? Could it, or an enhanced figure, enable the parent with care to take over the family home? How would that tie in with responsibility for any secured loan? Could continuity and stability for the children be achieved by continued occupancy of the family home even if it had to be sold at a specified time in future? Is the responsibility for the care of children having an impact on earning potential? Then look at s.9(1)(d). Has there been substantial dependence? Is retraining envisaged? If so, how long would it take? Finally, if provision under s.9(1)(c) or (d) in addition to fair sharing and any possible adjustment for financial advantage/disadvantage still leaves a very bleak outlook for the future, look at the possibility of the application of s.9(1)(e) as an alternative. Behaviour in general as well as in relation to economic consequences could be relevant for the last two principles. Any orders must also reasonable in light of current resources.

In *Little v. Little* and some other cases various different items of matrimonial property have been treated independently in the final disposal. Even so, having an accurate picture of the matrimonial assets and liabilities before considering the options can often widen the possibilities and allow more purposeful "reality testing". That in turn can defuse heightened emotions by enabling workable solutions to emerge rather than devoting energy to pursuing an outcome that may not be practicable. The costs involved in valuing property can be a deterrent. The expense of a surveyor, actuary and business valuer can be daunting. In many cases, however, independent input of this nature greatly assists a negotiated outcome.

Subs. (1)

Para. (a)

Fair sharing. Section 10 provides that "the net value of the matrimonial property shall be taken to be shared fairly between the parties of the marriage when it is shared equally or in such other proportions as are justified by special circumstances".

The same section defines "net value" as "the value of the property at the relevant date after deduction of any debts incurred by the parties or either of them—(a) before the marriage so far as they relate to the matrimonial property, and (b) during the marriage" and defines "matrimonial property" in subs. 4.

The calculation is not simply one of arithmetic. In *MacLachlan v. MacLachlan*, 1998 S.L.T. 693 Lord MacFadyen calculated the difference between the two pension funds of the parties. He noted that a "rigid application of equal sharing would require a small payment by the pursuer to the defender" and commented "that would amount to excessively fine tuning" (p. 697).

A number of issues have been raised by this principle: what is included in the definition of matrimonial property, the treatment of pension interests, the valuation of business interests, the impact of significant changes in value between the relevant date and the date of an order and the approach to "special circumstances" (with particular reference to the treatment of matrimonial property acquired from funds or assets not derived from the income or efforts of the parties during the marriage). These are dealt with in the notes to s.10. In general, two of the most common significant departures from equal sharing taking into account "special circumstances" have arisen from the use of matrimonial property as a family home and the source of funds invested in matrimonial property.

Para. (b)

Economic advantage/disadvantage. This is to be read along with subs. (2) and s.11(2).

This principle has taken some while to be used to any significant extent. It has been difficult to have it taken into account in a meaningful way in negotiation, but as it is increasingly aired in litigation (albeit with rather contradictory outcomes) it is more likely to be given weight in non-litigated outcomes. One of the problems is the difficulty in quantifying claims and assessing their strength. Because of the large number of sheriffs dealing with family actions there is little consistency in approach. Some wish arithmetical calculations and very detailed evidence, some accept a "broad brush" approach. The cost of contested litigation is very high. It can be difficult to obtain legal aid cover for expert evidence that may seem speculative.

See the notes to s.11(2) for specific application. Some of the issues that could be put forward under this heading have been considered under s.10(6) (special circumstances) and cases noted there may be of relevance. In terms of subs. (2) the economic advantage/disadvantage can arise and the contributions be made before or during the marriage.

There need be no matrimonial property for an award under this principle (*Dougan v. Dougan*, 1998 S.L.T.(Sh. Ct) 27).

Para. (c)

This should be read along with ss.8(1)(b) and (2), 11(3) and 13(2). It is necessary to look first of all at the possibility of a payment of capital or property transfer order then if necessary the possibility of a periodical allowance. Any order must be reasonable having regard to the resources of the parties. Although any aliment for the child is a factor to be taken into account this principle provides for additional financial payment to a spouse with the care of a child. The provisions of the Child Support Act 1991 have not superseded this principle (*Proctor v. Proctor*, 1994 G.W.D. 30–1814). Section 11(3) sets out the other factors to be taken into account. The principle has been applied in a number of cases. Orders granted have been for capital, periodical allowance or a mixture of both. In *Proctor* a small amount of capital and three years' periodical allowance was awarded. In *Monkman v. Monkman*, 1988 S.L.T.(Sh. Ct) 37 the wife had custody of a child aged nine. She had incurred outlays to give the child stability. The husband had no capital and little income. Periodical allowance was awarded for 10 years, not for future expenditure after the child was 16 but to spread over 10 years the burden undertaken by the wife until the child was 16. In *Peacock v. Peacock*, 1994 S.L.T. 40 the wife was awarded transfer of the home (with equity of about 15,000) and contents to look after the children aged 13 and 10. The husband received a policy with a surrender value of 643.75. He was unable to work. The wife had been working and maintaining the home and children. Sections 9(1)(a) and 10(6)(d) were stated to be the basis for the decision but the case seems relevant for s.9(1)(c). *MacLachlan v. MacLachlan*, 1998 S.L.T. 693 reinforced that it is justifiable, notwithstanding the provisions of the Child Support Act 1991, to depart from equal sharing to provide housing for children although in this particular case the availability of housing and interaction of ss.9(1)(a) and (c) balanced and no capital was awarded. It was also decided that it is inappropriate to use this principle to cover future school fees and rarely appropriate to use it to cover revenue expenses.

See the note to s.11(3) for further cases.

Para. (d)

Adjustment. The interaction of s.8(1)(b) and (2) and s.13(2) allows an order for periodical allowance under this principle but only if a capital payment or property transfer is inappropriate or insufficient and if it is reasonable having regard to the resources of the parties. There has to be averment and proof that capital would be insufficient (*Mackin v. Mackin*, 1991 S.L.T. (Sh. Ct) 22). The factors to be taken into account are set out in s.11(4).

It is important to bear in mind that three years is the *maximum* period for financial provision under this principle. There is no automatic three-year entitlement. Although the appropriate period should run from divorce it is common in negotiations for the time to run from the conclusion of an agreement between the parties. In that case the wording should be for a payment of aliment up to divorce and periodical allowance afterwards with provision for the possibility of variation by the court (or by arbitration if that were preferred). There have been some awards granted by the court for longer than three years stated to be justified under s.9(1)(d) for the first three years and s.9(1)(e) subsequently. This does seem inherently inconsistent since para. (d) is to allow for adjustment to not having support. If serious hardship is established and there is little prospect that support for up to three years will allow financial independence to develop, an award under para. (e) rather than para. (d) would seem appropriate.

In considering which principle to use it should be remembered that an award justified under s.9(1)(c) could be for longer than three years, depending on the age of the children.

An award can be made to operate at some point in the future. In *Shipton v. Shipton*, 1992 S.C.L.R. 23 a wife was awarded periodical allowance for three years, suspended until the husband obtained employment.

Orders for capital and periodical allowance can be made. In *Louden v. Louden*, 1994 S.L.T. 381 a wife was awarded 55 per cent of the capital and periodical allowance of 500 per month for one year to enable her to retrain.

See the note to s.11(4) for further cases.

Para. (e)

Hardship. As with s.9(1)(c) and (d), ss.8(1)(b) and (2) and 12(3) impose the need to eliminate the feasibility of a capital sum or property transfer order before an order for periodical allowance can be competent. It is less likely that sufficient capital will be available to meet a claim under this heading and orders tend to be for periodical allowance.

The factors to be considered are set out in s.11(5).

Although the idea of a "clean break" was much discussed as an objective of the Act this provision certainly leaves the door open to long-term financial support. The prospect of the divorce causing serious financial hardship must be proved but where that can be shown there is no necessary maximum time limit. Although most of the cases with open-ended support have been ones where the dependent spouse has had health problems this is not a factor in all such decisions. Refer to the note to s.11(5) for relevant cases.

Subs. (2)
See the note for s.9(1)(b).

Sharing of value of matrimonial property

10.—(1) In applying the principle set out in section 9(1)(a) of this Act, the net value of the matrimonial property shall be taken to be shared fairly between the parties to the marriage when it is shared equally or in such other proportions as are justified by special circumstances.

(2) The net value of the matrimonial property shall be the value of the property at the relevant date after deduction of any debts incurred by the parties or either of them—

(a) before the marriage so far as they relate to the matrimonial property, and

(b) during the marriage,
which are outstanding at that date.

(3) In this section "the relevant date" means whichever is the earlier of—

(a) subject to subsection (7) below, the date on which the parties ceased to cohabit;

(b) the date of service of the summons in the action for divorce.

(4) Subject to subsection (5) below, in this section and in section 11 of this Act "the matrimonial property" means all the property belonging to the parties or either of them at the relevant date which was acquired by them or him (otherwise than by way of gift or succession from a third party)—

(a) before the marriage for use by them as a family home or as furniture or plenishings for such home; or

(b) during the marriage but before the relevant date.

[1] (5) The proportion of any rights or interests of either party—

(a) under a life policy or similar arrangement; and

(b) in any benefits under a pension scheme which either party has or may have (including such benefits payable in respect of the death of either party), and

(c) in the assets in respect of which either party has accrued rights to benefits under a pension scheme
which is referable to the period to which subsection (4)(b) above refers shall be taken to form part of the matrimonial property.

[2] (5A) In the case of an unfunded pension scheme, the court may not make an order which would allow assets to be removed from the scheme earlier than would otherwise have been the case.

(6) In subsection (1) above "special circumstances", without prejudice to the generality of the words, may include—

(a) the terms of any agreement between the parties on the ownership or division of any of the matrimonial property;

(b) the source of the funds or assets used to acquire any of the matrimonial property where those funds or assets were not derived from the income or efforts of the parties during the marriage;

(c) any destruction, dissipation or alienation of property by either party;

(d) the nature of the matrimonial property, the use made of it (including use for business purposes or as a matrimonial home) and the extent to which it is reasonable to expect it to be realised or divided or used as security;

(e) the actual or prospective liability for any expenses of valuation or transfer of property in connection with the divorce.

(7) For the purposes of subsection (3) above no account shall be taken of any cessation of cohabitation where the parties thereafter resumed

cohabitation, except where the parties ceased to cohabit for a continuous period of 90 days or more before resuming cohabitation for a period or periods of less than 90 days in all.

[3] (8) The Secretary of State may by regulations make provision—

(a) for the value of any benefits under a pension scheme to be calculated and verified, for the purposes of this Act, in a prescribed manner;

(b) for the trustees or managers of any pension scheme to provide, for the purposes of this Act, information as to that value, and for the recovery of the administrative expenses of providing such information from either party,

and regulations made by virtue of paragraph (a) above may provide for that value to be calculated and verified in accordance with guidance which is prepared and from time to time revised by a prescribed body and approved by the Secretary of State.

[2] (9) Regulations under subsection (8) above shall be made by statutory instrument which shall be subject to annulment in pursuance of a resolution of either House of Parliament.

[2] (10) In this section—

"benefits under a pension scheme" includes any benefits by way of pension, whether under a pension scheme or not;

"pension scheme" means—

(a) an occupational pension scheme or a personal pension scheme (applying the definitions in section 1 of the Pension Schemes Act 1993, but as if the reference to employed earners in the definition of "personal pension scheme" were to any earners);

(b) a retirement annuity contract; or

(c) an annuity, or insurance policy, purchased or transferred for the purpose of giving effect to rights under a pension scheme falling within paragraph (a) above; and

"prescribed" means prescribed by regulations.

[2] (11) In this section, references to the trustees or managers of a pension scheme—

(a) in relation to a contract or annuity referred to in paragraph (b) or (c) of the definition of "pension scheme" in subsection (10) above, shall be read as references to the provider of the annuity;

(b) in relation to an insurance policy referred to in paragraph (c) of that definition, shall be read as a reference to the insurer.

NOTES
1. As amended by the Pensions Act 1995 (c. 26), s.167(2)(a) and by the Family Law Act 1996 (c. 27), s.17(a).
2. Inserted by the Family Law Act 1996 (c. 27), s.17(b).
3. Inserted by the Pensions Act 1995 (c. 26), s.167(2)(b).

DEFINITIONS
"action for divorce": s.17(2).
"cohabit": s.27(2).
"matrimonial property": s.10(4).
"party to the marriage": s.27(1).
"relevant date": s.10(3).

GENERAL NOTE

Subs. (1)
Special circumstances. These are expanded on in subs. (6). In *Lawson v. Lawson*, 1996 S.L.T.(Sh. Ct) 83 Sheriff Principal Nicholson commented "the reference to special circumstances' in s.10(1) does not qualify the way in which the net value of matrimonial property is to be determined. It simply introduces a factor of which account may be taken when a court is determining the division of matrimonial property of which the net value has been

determined". The starting point is the net value, then the next step is to consider whether special circumstances exist to justify a departure from equal sharing. The existence of special circumstances does not automatically lead to an unequal division (*Jacques v. Jacques*, 1997 S.L.T. 459).

Subs. (2)

Relevant date. This is defined in subs. (3).

Net value. Sheriff Thomson commented in *Shipton v. Shipton*, 1992 S.C.L.R. 23: "That value of any property varies according to the purpose for which the valuation is made is a familiar phenomenon. There also may be one value in theory and another in practice ... the Act, however, enjoins an equitable approach to the division of matrimonial property, and I think that a similar approach should be taken as regards its valuation" (p. 25). In that case, a debt due to the husband was substantially discounted because of the "parlous condition" of the liable company.

Debts due by the parties. The treatment of tax has arisen in a number of cases in calculating the net matrimonial property. In *Latter v. Latter*, 1990 S.L.T. 805 no allowance was made for notional capital gains tax in valuing a shareholding although such an allowance was made in *Bolton v. Bolton*, 1995 G.W.D. 14–799. In *Buchan v. Buchan*, 1992 S.C.L.R. 766 tax due by a self-employed fisherman was allowed to be deducted although not paid until after the relevant date. However in *McCormick v. McCormick*, 1994 S.C.L.R. 958 the husband wished to have estimated tax deducted from his business profits. As the tax was estimated and not payable immediately and as he paid tax in the ordinary way from year to year it was not allowed as a deduction. The decision in *McConnell v. McConnell*, 1997 Fam.L.R. 97 supports the approach of not taking into account notional tax on the valuation of an asset, but deducting as a debt tax liability which has arisen in relation to income received prior to the separation. (The subsequent appeal reported as *McConnell v. McConnell (No. 2)*, 1997 Fam.L.R. 108 did not reopen consideration of those issues.)

Discounts and penalties. Those which are potentially re-payable on resale of heritable property can be deducted in calculating the net value.

Case Law

Lawson v. Lawson, 1996 S.L.T.(Sh. Ct) 83. The value of a property purchased from the local authority was the market value less the discount potentially re-payable at the relevant date. (The earning of the discount by the husband prior to the marriage was not taken into account as matrimonial property.)

Mackin v. Mackin, 1991 S.L.T.(Sh. Ct) 22. The husband owned a house that he had purchased from his employers. There was a penalty if it were sold within five years. As the separation occurred within the five-year period the value as matrimonial property was the market value less penalty.

Subs. (3)

The relevant date can be of great significance. With or without malice, assets and liabilities can change significantly during a period of turbulence in a relationship. In certain pension schemes there comes a point when the value can increase dramatically over a relatively short time.

Para. (a)

Cessation of cohabitation. Periods of living apart are dealt with in subs. (7) but it can be necessary to establish a relevant date while the parties are still under the same roof. It may be claimed that prior to an action being served cohabitation had ceased. Section 27(2) provides that for the purposes of the Act, "the parties to a marriage shall be held to cohabit with one another only when they are in fact living together as man and wife". In *Buczynska v. Buczynski*, 1989 S.L.T. 558 the couple were still living under the same roof at the date of proof. Rather than taking the date of service of the initial writ as the relevant date it was held from the evidence that the relevant date was when the wife received a solicitor's letter asking her to leave. She then ceased to cook for, or sleep with, her husband. In *Brown v. Brown*, 1996 Fam.L.B. 23–9 and 1998 Fam.L.R. 81 the relevant date was taken to have been the date the wife contacted her solicitor, not when her husband decided the marriage was over as there was insufficient evidence of that decision in his behaviour. Sometimes a dispute over a relevant date involves a much bigger discrepancy between the parties' accounts. In *Mayor v. Mayor*, 1995 S.L.T. 1097 the husband claimed that after a (lengthy) period of separation there had been a reconciliation lasting almost eight months. The wife disputed that and her account was preferred.

Subs. (4)
The matrimonial property

Increase in value. Whether a particular asset falls within the definition of matrimonial property can be contentious. If an asset is excluded, a further issue has been raised as to whether an increase in its value could be treated as matrimonial property. In *Latter v. Latter*, 1990 S.L.T. 805 Lord Marnoch expressed the view that if an exclusion in relation to certain shares because they were gift had been appropriate he would have restricted this element to their value as the date of donation. That would have allowed any increase in value during the marriage to have been considered matrimonial property. This was not followed in *Whittome v. Whittome (No. 1)*, 1994 S.L.T. 114 where it was decided that the increase in value of non-matrimonial property is not matrimonial property. This does not preclude a claim based on financial advantage/disadvantage under s.9(1)(b), which could be quantified using the increase in value. This approach was considered in *Vance v. Vance*, 1997 S.L.T.(Sh. Ct) 71.

Business interests. Whether these are matrimonial property and, if so, how they should be valued are issues that arise frequently in negotiation and litigation. If one party is already involved in a partnership, as a shareholder in a limited company or as sole trader at the date of marriage the business could only become matrimonial property if it undergoes a significant restructuring after the marriage. In *Whittome v. Whittome (No. 1)*, 1994 S.L.T. 114 a gift of shares to the husband by a third party during the marriage was not considered matrimonial property; but neither was the bonus issue thereafter nor an increase in value through company reconstruction because the company maintained its original identity. Even if such assets cannot be brought within the definition of matrimonial property, a potential claim under s.9(1)(b) could be considered if the other spouse could establish that financial advantage had arisen because of either his or her contribution to the business itself or by taking responsibility for child care. This was explored in *Vance v. Vance*, 1997 S.L.T.(Sh. Ct) 71. In *Wilson v. Wilson*, 1998 S.C.L.R. 1103 a farming business run as a limited company was excluded from matrimonial property although it included assets acquired after the marriage and the husband was the main shareholder. An award was made on the basis of s.9(1)(b) (although there has been a reclaiming motion). In *Fulton v. Fulton*, 1998 S.L.T. 1262 the husband was a director in a limited company at the date of marriage then issued with shares after the marriage. The shareholding was included as matrimonial property.

The valuation of business interests for the purposes of the Act is complex. Specialist advice should be sought from an expert familiar with the legislation. Two broad approaches recur, net asset or future maintainable earnings. Where the particular and specialised skills of the spouse involved in the business form a large part of its value there seems more justification to focus on the asset value. A detailed consideration of the different approaches to business valuations can be found in *McConnell v. McConnell*, 1997 Fam.L.R. 97 where the net asset basis was favoured for a number of reasons including the fact that an earnings basis relied on the efforts of the defender (an architect) after the relevant date. *Crockett v. Crockett*, 1992 S.C.L.R. 591 used an earnings basis to value a butcher's business. Other cases dealing with business valuations include *Savage v. Savage*, 1997 Fam.L.R. 132 (a coachbuilder's business) and *Mayor v. Mayor*, 1995 S.L.T. 1097. In the last case a capital sum was awarded even though this would require the family business to be sold. Extract was superseded for a period of six months. In *Brown v. Brown*, 1998 Fam.L.R. 81 two businesses were involved with different considerations for each one. The question of goodwill was considered in *Rose v. Rose*, 1998 S.L.T.(Sh. Ct) 56 (aptly enough a flower and plant business) where the terms of a partnership agreement had a significant influence, and in *Bye v. Bye*, 1998 Fam.L.R. 103 (a business providing promotional displays). In both cases the value of goodwill was excluded.

Local authority discount. The entitlement to a discounted price for the purchase of a local authority house earned before marriage is not matrimonial property nor a special circumstance but the discount repayable at the relevant date falls to be deducted in calculating the net value (*Lawson v. Lawson*, 1996 S.L.T.(Sh. Ct) 83 and *Graham v. Graham*, 1997 G.W.D. 32–1631).

Damages. The timing of when the claim arises and is paid is fundamental. Even if it is matrimonial property s.10(6)(b) may have an impact.

Case Law
Petrie v. Petrie, 1988 S.C.L.R. 390. The husband was injured in an accident before the marriage and received substantial damages after the separation. The award was not matrimonial property.

Skarpass v. Skarpass, 1991 S.L.T.(Sh. Ct) 15 (appeal refused 1993 S.L.T. 343). An award of damages in respect of an injury sustained during the marriage was matrimonial property.

Louden v. Louden, 1994 S.L.T. 381. A husband's potential claim against his former employers for dismissal without required notice was matrimonial property.

CICB Awards. In the case of *McGuire v. McGuire C.B.*, 1991 S.L.T.(Sh. Ct) 76. An award was considered matrimonial property.

Redundancy payments. A redundancy payment made after the relevant date is not matrimonial property; although calculated by reference to past service it is for future loss and different from a pension (*Smith v. Smith*, 1989 S.L.T. 668 and *Tyrrell v. Tyrrell*, 1990 S.L.T. 406 and 1990 S.C.L.R. 244).

The fact that savings at the relevant date were derived from redundancy payment does not amount to a special circumstance (*Maclachlan v. Maclachlan*, 1998 S.L.T. 693).

Contents. Valuation of furniture and contents should be on a willing seller/buyer basis rather than a valuation based on auction room prices (*Latter v. Latter*, 1990 S.L.T. 805 and *Bolton v. Bolton*, 1995 G.W.D. 14–799).

It is within judicial knowledge that insurance valuations are more than a true and fair value of any item (*McConnell v. McConnell*, 1993 G.W.D. 34–2185).

Tax. In *MacRitchie v. MacRitchie*, 1994 S.C.L.R. 348—a refund of tax paid after the relevant date in respect of a prior over payment was considered matrimonial property.

Share Options. These are increasingly common. How should they be treated in terms of matrimonial property? An analogy could be drawn with pension rights or with damages. There does seem to be a good argument that some value should be attributed as matrimonial property. See Barr, A., "Share Options: Are They Matrimonial Property?", 1999 Fam.L.B. 39–3.

Otherwise than by way of gift or succession from a third party. The onus is on the party seeking to establish a case under s.10(4) (*Wilson v. Wilson*, 1998 S.C.L.R. 1103).

If gifted or inherited assets are retained in their original form then the issue will be proving the fact of the gift or inheritance. If a gift of money is provided to purchase a specific asset for one spouse it is likely that the asset will not be considered matrimonial property. In *Latter v. Latter*, 1990 S.L.T. 805 the purchase price of the matrimonial home was gifted by the wife's parents and the house was excluded from the matrimonial property. If gifted or inherited funds are reinvested in some completely new asset the new item will become matrimonial property. Section 10(6)(b) (source of funds) could be used to seek unequal sharing. If gifted or inherited assets simply undergo changes they may remain non-matrimonial property (*Whittome v. Whittome*, 1993 S.C.L.R. 137).

Para. (a)

For use as a family home. In *Buczynska v. Buczynski*, 1989 S.L.T. 558 a house purchased by the husband two years before the marriage was treated as matrimonial property. A link was made between the undoubted fact that the house was the matrimonial home in terms of the Matrimonial Homes (Family Protection) (Scotland) Act 1981 and its status as matrimonial property. Although s.27 of the 1985 Act does adopt the same meaning for the "matrimonial home" as s.22 of the 1981 Act, the phrase used in para. (a) is the "family home" *not* the "matrimonial home". Lord Morton did consider in any event that the property was acquired for use as a family home. An alternative approach was taken in *Ranaldi v. Ranaldi*, 1994 S.L.T.(Sh. Ct) 25 where a capital sum was awarded on the basis of the enhanced value of a house, which had not initially been a matrimonial home, but this approach was not taken in *Whittome v. Whittome*, 1993 S.C.L.R. 137 where it was decided that the increase in value of non-matrimonial property is not matrimonial property. A claim under s.9(1)(b) using the increase in value as a way of assessing financial advantage might well be appropriate in those circumstances.

Subs. (5)

Life policies. Different ways are being used to value policies. They can be valued by actuaries but this is seldom done. The surrender value can be requested at no cost. If a policy has a surrender value of around 6,000 or more a sale value can be obtained. If the policy was taken out before the date of marriage the value as matrimonial property has to be calculated. In *Tuke v. Tuke*, 1998 Fam.L.B. 31–3 the value at the date of marriage was deducted from the value at the relevant date rather than carrying out an apportionment. That approach does seem open to criticism (see Dr Nichols' comments in the case report). The formula for apportionment of pension interests set out in the Regulations is often used. The drawback there is that it does not allow for anything other than an even accrual. An actuarial valuation would clearly be the most scientific means.

Pensions. The inclusion of pension interests in matrimonial property has been one of the most radical aspects of the Act. It has disclosed both the significant value in some pension schemes and the dramatic disparity in the value of different schemes. The difference in the structure of the various pension schemes has also been highlighted. The existence of unfunded schemes led to the need for s.5A. Since, historically, women have tended to be in lower paid employment with much less generous pension provision, the right to claim a share of their husband's pension interests has corrected a wider economic imbalance for some women. The valuation of pension interests is dealt with from subs. (8) onwards and "earmarking" orders in s.12A. The approach to division is dealt with in the note to subs. (6)(d).

Forces pension. Apart from implications for valuation, which are covered in the note to subs. (8), the case of *Thomson v. Thomson*, 1991 S.C.L.R. 655 confirmed that an army pension does come within the definition of a pension scheme.

Pension in payment. A pension in payment does have a value as matrimonial property. A valuation by an actuary will be necessary. It is accepted as a capital rather than an income resource (*Gribb v. Gribb*, 1996 S.L.T. 719). Although accepted as a capital asset it has been recognised that in dealing with the value of a pension in payment the nature of the asset merits a departure from equal sharing (*Buckle v. Buckle*, 1995 S.C.L.R. 590).

Subs. (5A)
This has been inserted in anticipation of pension splitting, presumably to protect unfunded schemes.

Subs.(6)

Special circumstances
It was decided in *Jacques v. Jacques*, 1997 S.L.T. 459 that simply because special circumstances did exist the court was not required to effect an unequal division of the matrimonial property. Many decisions under this heading have been subject to criticism and it is one of the most difficult areas for advisers. The given list of potential special circumstances is not exhaustive—it "may include" those set out and others may be established. In *Farrell v. Farrell*, 1990 S.C.L.R. 717 the likelihood of an action of division and sale if no order was made, the pursuer having voluntarily paid the secured loan and the net value of the property at the relevant date being low constituted special circumstances. In *Collins v. Collins*, 1997 Fam.L.R. 50 the fact that the former matrimonial home had been adapted for the medical needs of the party wishing to remain there was treated as special circumstances. Many cases decided under this heading could have invoked s.9(1)(b) (financial advantage/disadvantage).

Para. (a)
Agreement
Bateman v. Bateman, 1994 G.W.D. 38–2234 unequal division was granted in favour of the wife because of special circumstances including the parties' agreement to keep their property separate.

Anderson v. Anderson, 1991 S.L.T. 11. The husband voluntarily gave "everything" to his wife at the time of separation and the Court declined to intervene on divorce. His action was considered principally as a gift or voluntary obligation but s.10(6)(a) was taken into account.

Toye v. Toye, 1992 S.C.L.R. 95. The husband agreed that his wife should stay in the family home so his share transferred to her, although this amounted to unequal sharing.

Webster v. Webster, 1992 G.W.D. 25–1432. The wife accepted that she should meet certain expenditure after separation so that was taken into account in division of assets.

Para. (b)
Source of funds
This provision has been applied in unpredictable ways, making it hard to advise clients. If the owner of non-matrimonial funds uses them in whole or part to acquire different assets in his or her own name before the relevant date the asset will become matrimonial property but the source of funds is more likely to be taken into account to justify unequal sharing in his or her favour than if invested in joint names.

In *Phillip v. Phillip*, 1988 S.C.L.R. 427 a quarter of the original price of the family home came from the sale of the house that the husband had owned prior to the marriage. The family home had been purchased in the husband's name. A quarter of the value at separation had been deducted from the assets before the remainder was divided equally. However in *McCormick v. McCormick*, 1994 G.W.D. 35–2078 the source of a shareholding derived from property inherited about 12 years before the relevant date was considered immaterial as it was considered that there was a limit as to how far it was appropriate to trace the sources of "matrimonial property" for the purposes of s.10(6)(b).

Where non-matrimonial property is invested in a joint asset it may be more difficult to establish a case under 10(6)(b). Special circumstances were accepted in *Kerrigan v. Kerrigan*, 1988 S.C.L.R. 603 where the husband's mother provided the deposit, the husband paid the secured loan and the cohabitation after the marriage was very brief.

In *Shipton v. Shipton*, 1992 S.C.L.R. 23 the exact amount of a loan or gift provided by the husband's father to purchase a plot of land some years before for the family home was taken into account in calculating the husband's share. The family home was in joint names. However, in *Bell* v. *Bell*, 1988 S.C.L.R. 457 the suggestion that money from shares inherited by the wife was invested in a jointly owned house was not considered as material to the consideration of "economic advantage" because the investment in joint property was treated as a gift of one half of the property. A similar approach was taken to an issue of gifted money raised in *McCormick* v. *McCormick*, 1994 G.W.D. 35–2078 (although in both of those cases the evidence appears to have been vague).

In *Jacques* v. *Jacques*, 1997 S.L.T. 459 the matrimonial home in joint names had been purchased with the proceeds of the sale of a house occupied prior to the relationship, in the husband's name. The Court of Session order for sale and equal division was allowed to stand.

If non-matrimonial funds are used towards the purchase of matrimonial property in joint names this may be interpreted as a gift or an agreement in terms of s.10(6)(a) and could defeat a source of funds argument under s.10(6)(b), as happened in *Jackson* v. *Jackson*, 1999 Fam.L.R. 108. This is not inevitable. In *R* v. *R* (Outer House, December 7, 1999, unreported), Lord Eassie, in upholding a source of funds argument, specifically remarked that equal division was intended to apply to the fruits of the parties' economic effort during the marriage.

Any case seeking to use s.10(6)(b) will have to be meticulously pled with a clear factual basis. If the funds were subsequently invested in joint property, intention and understanding at the time of purchase would have to be considered. Were there other deciding factors present—did lenders take both incomes into account or were matrimonial funds also invested in the joint property? Consideration should also be given to the use of s.9(1)(b). It would be inappropriate to try to track down every minor non matrimonial windfall. It is a different matter where significant funds which have not been generated by the parties' efforts or income during the marriage have been invested in matrimonial property.

Interaction with other principles. Budge v. *Budge*, 1990 S.L.T. 319. The husband's only capital was a croft which was his home and source of livelihood and which had been purchased from the sale of a cottage belonging to him and his first wife. His present wife had assisted him to run the croft and was awarded half the increase in value during the course of the marriage.

Jesner v. *Jesner*, 1992 S.L.T. 999. The wife was awarded 30 per cent of assets which originally all belonged to the husband to recognise the economic advantage he had gained.

Local authority tenancy discount on purchase. Lawson v. *Lawson*, 1996 S.L.T.(Sh. Ct) 83. The fact that the husband's tenancy prior to the marriage gave entitlement to a local authority discount was not accepted as a special circumstance under this paragraph.

Redundancy payments. MacLachlan v. *MacLachlan*, 1998 S.L.T. 693. The fact that savings at the relevant date were derived from a redundancy payment did not amount to a special circumstance.

Increase in value post relevant date. In *Buczynska* v. *Buczynski*, 1989 S.L.T. 558, *Wallis* v. *Wallis*, 1993 S.L.T. 1348 and *Dible* v. *Dible*, 1997 S.L.T. 787 the increase in the value of the matrimonial home between the relevant date and date of order was not accepted as a special circumstance. Although this was followed in *Welsh* v. *Welsh*, 1994 S.L.T. 828 the impact was balanced by the award of interest on the proportion of capital due to the wife in respect of her share of equity in the matrimonial home from the relevant date to the date of order for transfer.

Para. (c)
Destruction or dissipation of property
The courts are showing restraint in the use of this provision. Deliberate failure to pay a secured loan even though this resulted in repossession was not accepted as dissipation in *Park* v. *Park*, 1988 S.C.L.R. 584. Some definite action by the party was required before dissipation could be established. Losses arising from bad luck or judgment in business were not considered dissipation in *Russell* v. *Russell*, 1996 Fam.L.B. 21–5. However, in *Geddes* v. *Geddes*, 1991 G.W.D. 16–990 dissipation was not confined to matrimonial property and did not need to be deliberate. In *Goldie* v. *Goldie*, 1992 G.W.D. 21–1225 assets were divided equally after adding back 2,000 which the husband had dissipated from a loan for his own benefit. In *Short* v. *Short*, 1994 G.W.D. 21–1300 the wife had burdened the house with additional debt by forging her husband's signature. An equivalent amount was deducted from her half share.

Alienation of property
Jesner v. *Jesner*, 1992 S.L.T. 999. The fact that the husband had "contrived to lose the furnishings of the matrimonial home for all practical purposes" was regarded as special circumstances.

Para. (d)
Matrimonial home. The main use of this provision has been to allow the matrimonial home to continue to be used as the family home after divorce. It is interesting that there has been little use in litigation of the potential for occupancy rights in terms of s.14(2)(d). In *Cunniff* v. *Cunniff*, 1999 S.L.T. 992, Lord McCluskey commented on the fact that both parties expressly

excluded that option leaving the judge at first instance the stark choice of either putting the wife and child out of the home or transferring the property to the wife rendering the husband insolvent. The decision to transfer was upheld (which may make the gamble of staking everything on seeking transfer rather than occupancy rights more rather than less attractive!). A decision to transfer was made in *Cooper v. Cooper*, 1989 S.C.L.R. 347, *Farrell v. Farrell*, 1990 S.C.L.R. 717, *Peacock v. Peacock*, 1994 S.L.T. 40 (with a modest asset transferred to the husband in exchange) and *Clokie v. Clokie*, 1994 G.W.D. 3–149. In *Main v. Main*, 1990 S.C.L.R. 165 a straight transfer was refused but the wife was allowed more than equal sharing to allow her the possibility of buying out her husband's share to allow her to remain in the family home with the adult children. In *MacDonald v. MacDonald*, 1991 G.W.D. 31–1866 the husband had remained in the matrimonial home with the children and was paying the secured loan. He asked for transfer without consideration. The transfer was ordered but in exchange for one-half of the value, which the husband stated would mean the sale of the property. Transfer must be viable: it was refused in *Symon v. Symon*, 1991 S.C.L.R. 414 where neither party would have been able to pay the secured loan.

Business. Budge v. Budge, 1990 S.L.T. 319. Consideration was given to the fact that the only asset was a croft providing both home and livelihood for the husband and that a forced sale had been refused (although the wife was awarded capital based on increase in value during the marriage).

Davidson v. Davidson, 1994 S.L.T. 506. Unequal division was allowed in this case for a number of reasons including the fact that the farm which was part of the matrimonial property was being run by the wife as a business.

Pension. The fact that the value of the husband's pension was not realisable did not amount to "special circumstances" where there was no shortage of liquid assets (*Latter v. Latter*, 1990 S.L.T. 805, *McKenzie v. McKenzie*, 1991 S.L.T. 461 and *Brooks v. Brooks*, 1993 S.L.T. 184).

If there are no other liquid assets payment can be:
- deferred with interest (*Gulline v. Gulline*, 1992 S.L.T.(Sh.Ct) 71).
- deferred without interest (*Dorrian v. Dorrian*, 1991 S.C.L.R. 661).
- deferred and rounded up (*Bannon v. Bannon*, 1993 S.L.T. 999).
- made by instalments (*McEwan v. McEwan*, 1997 S.L.T. 118).

Factors that have modified awards include:
- shortage of liquid assets (*Muir v. Muir*, 1989 S.L.T.(Sh. Ct) 20).
- insecure financial circumstances (*Pryde v. Pryde*, 1991 S.L.T. 26).
- pension in payment (*Buckle v. Buckle*, 1995 S.C.L.R. 590).

The trend has been to make awards based on one-half of the value rather than a discounted amount and to make them payable immediately if there are other assets or at a later date with some enhancement if not, unless there are factors other than non-liquidity. The possibility of "earmarking" has proved fraught with difficulties and has not become a common route, but the introduction of "pension splitting" envisaged in the foreseeable future could have a more substantial impact.

Damages. Skarpass v. Skarpass, 1993 S.L.T. 343. Although personal injury awards of solatium and the future earnings were held to be matrimonial property they were discounted entirely under s.10(6)(b).

Para. (e)
Expenses

In *Farrell v. Farrell*, 1990 S.C.L.R. 717 a transfer to the wife was ordered while she had the benefit of legal aid.

Subs. (7)
Cessation of cohabitation

This elaborates on s.10(3) and can have a significant impact on the placing of the relevant date. In turn; that can have a significant impact on the net matrimonial property. It can also make its presence felt when calculating the period of separation for divorce. When a relationship starts to deteriorate there can be a number of trial separations. The relevant date in the circumstances will depend on how long the parties were apart and how long they were together in the period before the final separation. The issue was considered in *Pryde v. Pryde*, 1991 S.L.T.(Sh. Ct) 26 where the couple separated in March, attempted a reconciliation in June, then separated finally in August. The relevant date was taken to have been August. The report is not precise about the dates. On the broad information given the initial separation could have been for more than 90 days and the period of reconciliation less than 90 but presumably the specific dates created different arithmetic. Doubt was cast on the clarity of the wording of s.10(7) in this case, but the subsection does set out that the relevant date will only be "backdated" where a couple stop living together for a consecutive period of 90 days or more, then live together again for less than 90 days in total.

Subs. (8)
Valuation of pension benefits
　　After a rather bumpy start in dealing with very new territory the main issues that emerged were whether the valuation should be on the basis of the member continuing in service or leaving service and whether the value of the potential widow's or widower's benefit should be included. The subsequent amendment to s.10(5)(b), including benefits payable in respect of the death of either party (*i.e.* including the widow's or widower's benefit) and the provision for the making of regulations for the calculation of an appropriate valuation, seemed set to simplify matters. Regulation 3 of the Divorce etc. (Pensions) (Scotland) Regulations 1996 (S.I. 1996 No. 1901) duly prescribed the cash equivalent, the leaving service approach in almost all cases and the use of a straightforward time-based apportionment to ascertain the value for the relevant period. In *George v. George*, 1991 S.L.T.(Sh. Ct) 8 the importance of evidence of value had been stressed. At first it was thought that the Regulations would mean that for divorce actions beginning on or after August 19, 1996 the cash equivalent transfer value (CETV) provided by the pension scheme would be adequate and actuarial input no longer necessary (except in cases where the pension was already in payment or for those within one year of normal pension age). (In appropriate cases the CETV is to be supplied within three months (reg. 4(1).)
　　It was then suggested that although the CETV provided by the pension scheme will be appropriate in many cases it may not truly reflect the value as matrimonial property for a number of schemes. Because of the structure of the pension schemes for the police, prison service, fire service and armed forces it has been argued that the CETV is not a proper assessment of their value for the purposes of the Act and a different approach has been suggested giving something closer to the "replacement" value (see Eden, S., "Pensions and Divorce", 1996 Fam.L.B. 23–3 and Smith, S., "Valuation of Pension Rights on Divorce", 1999 Fam.L.B. 38–3). There is a strong argument from others, including pensions specialist Iain Talman, a Glasgow solicitor and Dr E. Clive (*Husband and Wife* (4th ed.), p. 455, fn. 19), that the wording of the Regulations is quite clear in imposing the transfer value. This is an issue that will no doubt be tested and the subject of reported decisions. A plea to the relevance of averments simply narrating an actuarial valuation has been upheld. The sheriff indicated that "the discretion available to the court in terms of the regulations is very much in the context of the calculation of the cash equivalent sum being established ... It might, in certain cases, be feasible for the pursuer to state the amount of the cash equivalent fund and then, by averment, set out why it does not provide a fair value" (*Miller v. Miller*, June 9, 1999, Ayr Sheriff Court, unreported). There are assumptions made within a transfer value and so there could be a range of possible transfer values. This would be over a significantly smaller band of possibility. It may be worth having expert advice where there are discretionary benefits or where the member has serious health problems. It is also important to check whether there are additional voluntary contributions (AVCs). To approach the total value of the pension rights over the time of the marriage, the value of the pension at the relevant date should be divided by the total period of membership of the scheme before the relevant date and multiplied by the period after the marriage and prior to the relevant date the party was a member of the scheme.

Subs. 10
　　Benefits under a pension scheme. It appears that State earnings related pensions (SERPS) are included although some doubt has been expressed by some pensions experts. The DSS will provide a notional capitalised valuation of SERPS rights on request.

S.I.s ISSUED UNDER SECTION
　　Divorce etc. (Pensions) (Scotland) Regulations S.I. 1996 No. 1901.
　　Divorce etc. (Pensions) (Scotland) Amendment Regulations S.I. 1997 No. 745.

Factors to be taken into account

　　11.—(1) In applying the principles set out in section 9 of this Act, the following provisions of this section shall have effect.
　　(2) For the purposes of section 9(1)(b) of this Act, the court shall have regard to the extent to which—
　　　(a) the economic advantages or disadvantages sustained by either party

have been balanced by the economic advantages or disadvantages sustained by the other party, and

(b) any resulting imbalance has been or will be corrected by a sharing of the value of the matrimonial property or otherwise.

(3) For the purposes of section 9(1)(c) of this Act, the court shall have regard to—

(a) any decree or arrangement for aliment for the child;
(b) any expenditure or loss of earning capacity caused by the need to care for the child;
(c) the need to provide suitable accommodation for the child;
(d) the age and health of the child;
(e) the educational, financial and other circumstances of the child;
(f) the availability and cost of suitable child-care facilities or services;
(g) the needs and resources of the parties; and
(h) all the other circumstances of the case.

(4) For the purposes of section 9(1)(d) of this Act, the court shall have regard to—

(a) the age, health and earning capacity of the party who is claiming the financial provision;
(b) the duration and extent of the dependence of that party prior to divorce;
(c) any intention of that party to undertake a course of education or training;
(d) the needs and resources of the parties; and
(e) all the other circumstances of the case.

(5) For the purposes of section 9(1)(e) of this Act, the court shall have regard to—

(a) the age, health and earning capacity of the party who is claiming the financial provision;
(b) the duration of the marriage;
(c) the standard of living of the parties during the marriage;
(d) the needs and resources of the parties; and
(e) all the other circumstances of the case.

(6) In having regard under subsections (3) to (5) above to all the other circumstances of the case, the court may, if it thinks fit, take account of any support, financial or otherwise, given by the party who is to make the financial provision to any person whom he maintains as a dependant in his household whether or not he owes an obligation of aliment to that person.

(7) In applying the principles set out in section 9 of this Act, the court shall not take account of the conduct of either party unless—

(a) the conduct has adversely affected the financial resources which are relevant to the decision of the court on a claim for financial provision; or
(b) in relation to section 9(1)(d) or (e), it would be manifestly inequitable to leave the conduct out of account.

DEFINITIONS
"child": s.27(1).
"the court": s.27(1).
"matrimonial property": s.10(4).
"needs": s.27(1).
"obligation of aliment": ss.1(2) and 27(1).
"party to a marriage": s.27(1).
"resources": s.27(1).

GENERAL NOTE
Section 10 elaborates on s.9(1)(a). Section 11 sets out the factors for the remaining four principles. Subsection (7)(a) applies to all five s.9 principles, while subs. (7)(b) applies only to s.9(1)(d) or (e). The notes for appropriate paragraph of s.9 should also be taken into account.

Subs. (2)

Economic advantage/disadvantage

This should be read along with s.9(1)(b) and (2), and subs. (7)(a).

In *De Winton v. De Winton*, 1996 G.W.D. 29–1752 the Lord Ordinary stated that "the Court must identify all the economic advantages derived by either party from the contributions of the other and all the economic disadvantages suffered by either party in the interests of the other or of the family. Thereafter upon consideration of that balancing exercise the Court can determine whether an order should be made." He also noted "it is plain from the interaction between section 9(1)(b) and section 11(2) that it is only where there is an imbalance that the court can then go further to consider what order is called for." In this case an award was made on the basis of economic advantage gained by the husband from his wife's financial investment in their farming partnership. In *R v. R* (Outer House, December 7, 1999, unreported), Lord Eassie accepted that financial disadvantage had been suffered and commented that detailed accountancy evidence was not necessary, stating that "(o)ne in effect recognises the inability of the wife to follow up an independent economic activity because of her maternal and marital responsibilities." The terms of s.9(2) made it clear that the period prior to the marriage can be taken into account but what of the period after the divorce? Considering that point in *Cahill v. Cahill*, 1998 S.L.T. 96 the sheriff principal observed that "if earning capacity becomes disadvantaged in the course of the marriage I have difficulty in seeing how that loss can be evaluated except by reference to an extended period of time part of which may be after the dissolution of the marriage" (p. 99G). He doubted *Dougan v. Dougan*, 1998 S.L.T.(Sh. Ct) 27 on this point.

Some of the cases decided taking into account special circumstances under ss.9(1)(a) and 10(6) could have been considered under this principle and may be of relevance. Sometimes it is not clear which principle has been relied on.

Although more than one factor is often taken into account some themes have emerged. However, there has been little harmony in their development.

Career. To succeed on this basis it is important to have clear factual evidence about the career which was interrupted, the prognosis for "re-entry" and the consequent economic loss. An award is not likely to be justified if the work relinquished was not well paid with no career structure and can easily be taken up again, and where the standard of living during the cohabitation was good.

Petrie v. Petrie, 1988 S.C.L.R. 390. A wife had been, prior to the cohabitation, a single parent supporting her two children from her own earnings and as a result of the cohabitation was able to give up work and be supported for at least part of the period at a higher level than before.

Luckwell v. Luckwell, 1992 G.W.D. 34–2005. It was accepted that the wife now aged 64 suffered economic disadvantage because the remote area in which the couple lived had prevented her from taking employment during the marriage and the family home was transferred to her even though that gave her 60 per cent of the matrimonial property.

Clokie v. Clokie, 1993 G.W.D. 16–1059 and 1994 G.W.D. 3–149. An unequal division of assets was awarded to the wife who had prejudiced her career to further her husband's.

McCormick v. McCormick, 1994 G.W.D. 35–2078. The matrimonial home was transferred to the wife (although worth more than half of the net matrimonial property) for reasons including the fact that she had given up her career as a midwife to care for the husband and children and would continue to be disadvantaged in securing regular employment.

Louden v. Louden, 1994 S.L.T. 381. The wife's disadvantage in career terms was not considered sufficiently balanced by the contribution of the husband during the marriage and she was awarded 55 per cent of net matrimonial property. Both s.9(1)(b) and (d) appear to have been taken into account.

Increase in value of matrimonial home post separation. Wallis v. Wallis, 1993 S.L.T. 1348 decided that an increase in value between separation and divorce is not in itself a special circumstance under s.10(1). The decision gave rise to much debate. The proposals in the 1999 Discussion Paper would make the value on transfer the value at the date of the order rather than the relevant date. Use of s.14(2)(j) to seek interest payable from the relevant date could redress potential imbalance. There could be an argument under s.9(1)(b) if the other party had made any contribution to the matrimonial home during the separation.

Phillip v. Phillip, 1988 S.C.L.R. 427. The husband occupied the family home for 12 years between separation and divorce and paid nothing to his wife. Although it was accepted that he was advantaged, this was not from the contribution of his wife so s.9(1)(b) did not apply. It was observed that the wife could have claimed interest from the date of separation.

Muir v. Muir, 1989 S.C.L.R. 445. The matrimonial home and endowment policies increased in value between separation and divorce but again, as the wife had made no contribution to the increased value, there was no scope to invoke s.9(1)(b). However, the increased value was taken into account as a resource in assessing the ability to pay.

Payments of secured loan. There have been a variety of ways of dealing with payments of the secured loan after separation. There has been no consistent approach where the party in occupation pays the secured loan with no contribution from the other. If one parent is in the matrimonial home with the children and the other parent pays the secured loan this may well be seen as part of alimentary provision rather than an advantage to the other parent.

Kerrigan v. Kerrigan, 1988 S.C.L.R. 603. It was decided that the wife had obtained economic advantage from her husband's payments of the secured loan. There was a consequent increase in the value of the jointly owned matrimonial home. The husband's mother's contribution of the deposit was another factor. The house was transferred to him although worth more than one-half of the value of the net matrimonial property.

Farrell v. Farrell, 1990 S.C.L.R. 717. The wife remained in the jointly owned matrimonial home and voluntarily paid the secured loan. There were no liquid assets. She was awarded transfer of title to the home, the related policy and a capital sum based on the husband's share of the joint liability in relation to the home that she had met during the period of separation. Although the decision specifically mentioned special circumstances under s.10, an argument was also advanced under s.9(1)(b). The fact that the wife had enjoyed the benefit of occupation and would presumably have had housing costs to meet one way or another did not appear to be taken into account. The value of the property at the date of proof was not stated. If it had increased in value the husband appears to have been found liable to compensate his wife for outlays in respect of an appreciating asset without either having had the benefit of ownership or potential credit for the increase in value. The transfer of title and policy seemed clearly justified. The award of a capital sum in addition may well have gone beyond the scope of s.9(1)(b). Contrast *Lewis v. Lewis,* 1993 S.C.L.R. 32. Where a house sale was ordered with equal division although the wife who was resident in the house had paid the secured loan and received no aliment from the husband, and *McKenzie v. McKenzie,* 1991 S.L.T. 461. The wife occupied the house during the period of separation but the husband paid the secured loan. This was considered a regulation of aliment rather than something to be reflected in a capital division.

Non-financial contribution to matrimonial home. In *Jesner v. Jesner,* 1992 S.L.T. 999 the wife's contribution in looking after the family home and caring for the family was considered to have given an economic advantage to the husband. As a result, she was awarded 30 per cent of the assets although they had all originally been the husband's. On the other hand, in *Welsh v. Welsh,* 1994 S.L.T. 828 and in *Adams v. Adams (No. 1),* 1997 S.L.T. 144 economic disadvantages suffered by the wife as a result of bringing up the children were considered to have been balanced out by the husband's financial contribution to the household.

Non-matrimonial assets including business interests. Ranaldi v. Ranaldi, 1994 S.L.T.(Sh. Ct) 25. The wife was awarded a sum representing half of the enhancement in the value of a boarding house (not matrimonial property) during marriage because she helped to run the business and brought up the children.

Davidson v. Davidson, 1994 S.L.T. 506. Various factors operated to lead to unequal division in favour of the wife. One of these factors was the wife's gifts to her husband's business before and during the marriage which gave him an economic advantage to her disadvantage.

Vance v. Vance, 1997 S.L.T.(Sh. Ct) 71. Proof was allowed to explore the possible increase in the value of the husband's business (non-matrimonial property) from profits which may have been retained to allow consideration of whether the wife might have contributed.

Cahill v. Cahill, 1998 S.L.T.(Sh. Ct) 96. The husband carried out improvement work to a cottage belonging to his wife which did not form part of the matrimonial property. A capital sum was awarded because of the future financial advantage to her.

Wilson v. Wilson, 1998 S.C.L.R. 1103. Although the husband's farming business was excluded as matrimonial property an award was made under s.9(1)(b). Her lifestyle during the marriage was affected by the profits being retained in the company and so the wife had not had a "balancing" advantage during the marriage.

Boyes v. Boyes, 1996 Fam.L.B. 20–6. The wife was accepted as having suffered disadvantage where money she inherited was spent on the family before the relevant date.

No matrimonial property. There need be no matrimonial property at all for an award to be made under this principle as long as there has been financial disadvantage.

De Winton v. De Winton, 1997 S.L.T. 1118. Each party had substantial non-matrimonial property and the husband had sustained advantage from the wife's contribution, so a capital sum was awarded even though there was no matrimonial property from which the imbalance could be corrected.

Dougan v. Dougan, 1998 S.L.T.(Sh. Ct) 27 the wife took up part-time lower paid work after the marriage and an award of capital made although there were no matrimonial assets from which it could paid. (It was stated that account could only be taken of disadvantage up to but not beyond divorce, although that was doubted in *Cahill v. Cahill,* 1998 S.L.T.(Sh. Ct) 96.)

Financial Prudence. Macdonald v. Macdonald, 1994 G.W.D. 7–404. An unequal division of capital was awarded to the wife who had contributed a high proportion of her resources to necessary family expenditure, in contrast with the husband's personal extravagance (this was described as "special circumstances" but could be of relevance for s.9(1)(b)).

Other financial obligations. Hunter v. Hunter, 1996 S.C.L.R. 329. An argument that the husband's obligation to aliment children from a previous marriage caused the wife disadvantage was rejected.

Tahir v. Tahir (No. 2), 1995 S.L.T. 451. The husband took jewellery from his wife to his advantage and her disadvantage, and her capital sum was increased to take that into account.

Subs. (3)

This should be read along with s.9(1)(c) and subs. (7)(a).

It should be remembered that this principle is to supplement, not replace, a parent's duty to aliment children.

Para. (a)

MacLachlan v. MacLachlan, 1998 S.L.T. 693 confirmed that the Child Support Act provisions do not supersede this principle but in so doing made particular reference to the potential capital aspect of s.9(1)(c). Initially the formula introduced by the child support regulations included an element for the carer, based on income support rates. Subsequent amendments have reduced the amount to be taken into account for the carer where there is no qualifying child under 11.

Para. (b)

Russell v. Russell, 1996 Fam.L.B. 21–5 the husband was caring for the children and the wife's share of capital was reduced as for the foreseeable future the husband would have to look after the children without any assistance from her.

Para. (c)

McDevitt v. McDevitt, 1988 S.C.L.R. 206 the wife who was unemployed had custody of one child and residential access to the other two. She was awarded periodical allowance for three years to maintain a home for residential access.

Murley v. Murley, 1995 S.C.L.R. 1138. Title to the matrimonial home was transferred to the wife to allow it to remain as the family home, but an order was also granted for a standard security to be granted in favour of the husband to the extent of 50 per cent of the advantage gained by the wife.

MacLachlan v. MacLachlan, 1998 S.L.T. 693. The wife was allowed additional capital because of her need for larger accommodation for the children.

Subs. (4)

This should be read along with s.9(1)(d), subs. (7)(b) and s.13 subss (1) and (2).

With so many factors interweaving it is difficult to ascertain any clear strands. The more factors that are brought into play the stronger the claim. Some examples are:

Para. (a)
Age, health and earning capacity

Park v. Park, 1988 S.C.L.R. 584. A wife who had been married for five years and was now earning 5,040 per annum was awarded periodical allowance from a husband earning 20,600 per annum at the rate of 70 per week for one year then 35 for one further year. The arithmetic was on the basis of aiming to provide the wife with one-third of the joint income initially, rather than taking a detailed look at her outgoings.

Barclay v. Barclay, 1991 S.C.L.R. 205. A couple in their late twenties had been married and living together for three years then separated for four years. A separation agreement gave the wife capital and 15 per week for an unspecified period. The wife had multiple sclerosis and her condition had deteriorated. If no periodical allowance was awarded her means tested benefit would increase correspondingly so that there was no "hardship" under s.9(1)(e) but a three-year periodical allowance of 15 per week was awarded under s.9(1)(b).

Para. (b)
Duration and extent of dependence

Petrie v. Petrie, 1988 S.C.L.R. 390. The wife (aged 42) and the husband had cohabited for five years prior to their two-year marriage. The whole period was taken as relevant in determining the wife's dependence, which was total. She had no qualifications for employment, an order for capital was considered inappropriate as the disabled husband was dependent on income from invested capital and a periodical allowance was awarded for one year to enable the wife to seek employment.

Sheret v. Sheret, 1990 S.C.L.R. 799. The husband was a sailor who supported his wife , aged

43, when ashore but not while at sea which accounted for half of their two-year marriage. Periodical allowance was awarded for 13 weeks.

Tyrrell v. Tyrrell, 1990 S.L.T. 406. A wife who had been alimented throughout the seven years of separation and now had a part-time job was awarded periodical allowance for one more year to adjust.

Dever v. Dever, 1988 S.C.L.R. 352. A wife aged 27, married and cohabiting for six years and now on state benefits was awarded periodical allowance from her husband who had supported her throughout the marriage, but it was restricted to six months as she had shown the capacity to survive without his help for 18 months since the separation, *cf. Gray v. Gray*, 1991 S.C.L.R. 422. As the wife was considered to have already adjusted her life in style since the separation seven years earlier she was considered no longer to be dependent and no award of periodical allowance was made.

Para. (c)

Intention to undertake education or training

Louden v. Louden, 1994 S.L.T. 381. It was held to be permissible to award capital as well as periodical allowance to allow a wife to retrain.

Toye v. Toye, 1992 S.C.L.R. 95. The wife (aged 48) was provided with periodical allowance for three years to allow her to cover the cost of the family home being transferred to her until the 13-year-old daughter was 16 and to allow an opportunity for the wife to take steps to retrain—a mix of s.9(1)(c) and (d).

Para. (d)

Needs and resources

Atkinson v. Atkinson, 1988 S.C.L.R. 396. The husband made a generous capital settlement and was alimenting their child. On appeal periodical allowance was limited to three years (rather than being made without limitation of time).

Para. (e)

All the other circumstances of the case

McKenzie v. McKenzie, 1991 S.L.T. 461. Awarding periodical allowance for three years under s.9(1)(d) and then indefinitely under s.9(1)(e) was considered fairer to a husband with substantial income than awarding capital in lieu. There seems an inherent inconsistency in making an award straddle paras (d) and (e).

Subs. (5)

This is to be read along with s.9(1)(e), subs. (7)(a) and (b) and s.13(2).

In the cases where an award has been made under this heading more than one factor outlined has been present and the awards have been for varying periods of time. There must be a prospect of the divorce causing serious financial hardship but where that can be shown there is no necessary maximum time limit. Although most of the cases with open-ended support have been ones where the claimant had health problems, this has not been a factor in all such decisions. Some cases have included support for three years under s.9(1)(d) followed by a further period of support under s.9(1)(e). Since the basis of the award in each case would appear to be inconsistent there does seem to be an argument that any award for longer than three years, unless justified by s.9(1)(c), would really need to be justified under s.9(1)(e) and based only on that principle. A long time married claimant with health problems which would restrict potential employment who will not receive enough capital to provide income may succeed on an open-ended basis (unless the payer will have a significantly reduced income on retirement). However, a claim arising from a long marriage where the claimant devoted her time to the family and at the time of claim has little real prospect of obtaining adequately paid employment because of her age and lack of up-to-date qualifications may also have a prospect of success if there is insufficient capital to provide income and the husband is well paid. Some examples are:

(a) Granted—unlimited time

Johnstone v. Johnstone, 1990 S.L.T.(Sh. Ct) 79. The wife was aged 35 and unable to work because of her epilepsy. There was one child. The couple had been married and lived together for 13 years. The wife was awarded periodical allowance of 100 per month until her death or remarriage.

McKenzie v. McKenzie, 1991 S.L.T. 461. A couple who were married and had been together for 16 years. There were no dependent children. The wife ran a small business but had very little income from it. She would be entitled to a small pension at 60. She was awarded a capital sum. It was accepted that she was likely to be short of money despite the capital. Periodical allowance was awarded for three years under s.9(1)(d) and then indefinitely under s.9(1)(e). It was taken into account that capital was tied up in property and it was considered fairer for the husband, who had substantial income, to pay long-term support rather than capital in lieu.

Haugan v. Haugan, 1996 S.L.T. 321. The wife was 51 years old and had been married and lived with her husband for about 26 years. She had various health problems including mental health problems and a very restricted earning capacity. She was found entitled to periodical allowance under this heading until her death or remarriage.

(b) *Granted—specific period*

Stott v. Stott, 1987 G.W.D. 17–645. The wife was aged 42 and the couple had been married for 24 years. The husband had a steady income but no capital. The wife had a low income and no training. Periodical allowance was awarded for three years under s.9(1)(d) and then a smaller weekly payment for another four years under s.9(1)(e).

Bell v. Bell, 1988 S.C.L.R. 457. The wife was aged 51 and had been married and living with her husband for 26 years. She was a qualified teacher but had devoted her time to bringing up the children. She was dependent on her husband's financial support throughout the marriage and was not likely to find any reasonably paid work. Her capital allowed her to have a house but no income. Periodical allowance was awarded until the husband (then aged 53) retired at 60 or until her own earlier death or remarriage.

(c) *Refused*

Murray v. Murray, 1993 G.W.D. 16–1058. A 56-year-old wife had part-time work available to her and she would be entitled to a small pension at 60. She was awarded two years' periodical allowance under s.9(1)(d). It was not accepted that she was likely to suffer serious financial hardship and so no award was made under s.9(1)(e).

Bolton v. Bolton, 1995 G.W.D. 14–799. The 60-year-old wife had lived with her husband for over 33 years. The couple had a high standard of living. The wife had not worked during the separation due to stress and then arthritis in her spine and had no prospect of employment. She did receive a significant amount of capital and had some non-matrimonial resources and was not awarded any periodical allowance under s.9(1)(e). She was awarded periodical allowance for the relatively short period up until payment of the capital sum.

Subs. (7)

Para. (a)

There is some overlap with the provision for "special circumstances" in terms of s.10(6)(c) (destruction, dissipation or alienation of property by either party) and the cases noted there could have relevance for this paragraph. The fair sharing, balancing of capital resources and sharing responsibility for childcare is to be carried out regardless of matrimonial fault unless the fault directly affected the finances.

In *Collins v. Collins*, 1997 Fam.L.R. 50 the conduct of the wife in refusing money offered during negotiations which was only available at that point was taken as adversely affecting the financial resources.

Para. (b)

A routine general assessment of the ethical or moral behaviour of the parties is ruled out. Considering the "economic practicalities rather than the attribution of fault" was determined as the basis of financial provision in *White v. White*, 1990 G.W.D. 12–616. This can come as something of a shock to a spouse who believes him- or herself to have been wronged. For an adviser to acknowledge that shock (without reinforcing it) can be crucial in allowing negotiations to proceed. If the legal information comes across as a denial of the strong feelings it might simply be rejected in response. The client's energy will remain locked into the strong negative feelings rather than moving into future planning. After appropriate acknowledgment can come acceptance and problem solving.

Subsequent cohabitation

In *Brunton v. Brunton*, 1986 S.L.T. 49 an award of interim aliment was reduced to nil because the recipient was living with a new partner and receiving state benefit. However, this was distinguished in *Kavanagh v. Kavanagh*, 1989 S.L.T. 134 where it was emphasised that it "cannot be a strict rule of law that the fact that an ex-wife is living with another man who is not supporting her, renders a continued award of periodical allowance incompetent" (p. 135C).

Orders for payment of capital sum or transfer of property

12.—(1) An order under section 8(2) of this Act for payment of a capital sum or transfer of property may be made—

    (a) on granting decree of divorce; or

(b) within such period as the court on granting decree of divorce may specify.

(2) The court, on making an order referred to in subsection (1) above, may stipulate that it shall come into effect at a specified future date.

(3) The court, on making an order under section 8(2) of this Act for payment of a capital sum, may order that the capital sum shall be payable by instalments.

(4) Where an order referred to in subsection (1) above has been made, the court may, on an application by either party to the marriage on a material change of circumstances, vary the date or method of payment of the capital sum or the date of transfer of property.

DEFINITIONS
"the court": s.27(1).
"decree of divorce": s.17(2).
"party to a marriage": s.27(1).
"property": s.27(1).

GENERAL NOTE
This deals with the timing of and method for payment of a capital sum or transfer of property. Section 12(1)(b) allows a divorce to be granted while reserving the making of orders for capital or transfer at a later date. Although those orders would have to be craved in the process by the time divorce was granted and there could be some particular urgency for the divorce itself, there does seem merit in having the financial issues settled by the time divorce is granted. It allows the family to be clear where they stand. It prevents a possible collision between family law and the law of succession. The overwhelming preponderance of orders are made on the granting of decree of divorce either with immediate effect or by deferred or instalment payments. Since only a minority of cases are dealt with by litigation and the majority by negotiation it is extremely unusual for a divorce to be granted without the financial aspects having been resolved.

The section reinforces the fact that orders must be a justified by the s.9 principles and be reasonable having regard to the resources of parties in terms of s.8(2).

Subs. (1)
Para. (b)
An example of a case in which divorce was granted and the financial issues reserved is *Mackin v. Mackin*, 1991 S.L.T.(Sh. Ct) 22 where the divorce was granted in November and the proof ordered the following January. The proof was adjourned more than once due to pressure of business. Interim spousal aliment was considered competent (though none awarded) in *Neill v. Neill*, 1987 S.L.T.(Sh. Ct) 143 when decree of divorce was granted and the case continued in relation to financial provision. In *Muir v. Muir*, 1994 S.C.L.R. 178 a decree of divorce was granted and the making of financial orders postponed. That case also underlined the need for a crave for any financial orders proving the truth of the adage "if you don't ask, you don't get!".

Subs. (2)
There is an argument that the date could be following the happening of a specified future event rather than an actual date set down at the time of the order. This line was not accepted in *Geddes v. Geddes*, 1991 G.W.D. 16–990 but was followed in *Symon v. Symon*, 1991 S.C.L.R. 414 where payment was postponed until a date one month after the sale of the parties' house (the sale to proceed no later than six months after the order). It seems quite appropriate to link the date of effectiveness of an order to definite future events.

Little v. Little, 1990 S.L.T. 785. One half of the capital sum was payable immediately and payment of the balance deferred for a period of six years.

Shand v. Shand, 1994 S.L.T. 387. Payment was deferred for two years to allow the defender time to realise or otherwise obtain funds.

In *Collins v. Collins*, 1997 Fam.L.R. 50 payment of the capital sum was deferred until the death of the husband who was having the matrimonial home transferred to him.

Subss. (3) and (4)
There is an attraction in seeking a capital sum payable by instalments in terms of subs. (3) rather than a periodical allowance in terms of s.13 where an order is justified by s.9(1)(c), (d) or (e) since although variation of a capital sum is allowed in terms of subs. (4) it is only as to date

or method of payment, whereas variation of periodical allowance under s.13(4) could allow a downward variation or recall of the order. However that is likely to have the effect of making provision arising from future rather than past events effectively payable as capital from income with only limited provision for review. It does not seem in keeping with the purpose of s.9(1)(c), (d) and (e)—see the note to s.13. An instalment order can be made payable from a state benefit (*Gray v. Gray*, 1999 G.W.D. 38–1852).

Orders for payment of capital sum: pensions lump sums

[1] **12A.**—(1) This section applies where the court makes an order under section 8(2) of this Act for payment of a capital sum (a "capital sum order") by a party to the marriage ("the liable party") in circumstances where—

  (a) the matrimonial property within the meaning of section 10 of this Act includes any rights or interests in benefits under a pension scheme which the liable party has or may have (whether such benefits are payable to him or in respect of his death); and

  (b) those benefits include a lump sum payable to him or in respect of his death.

(2) Where the benefits referred to in subsection (1) above include a lump sum payable to the liable party, the court, on making the capital sum order, may make an order requiring the trustees or managers of the pension scheme in question to pay the whole or part of that sum, when it becomes due, to the other party to the marriage ("the other party").

(3) Where the benefits referred to in subsection (1) above include a lump sum payable in respect of the death of the liable party, the court, on making the capital sum order, may make an order—

  (a) if the trustees or managers of the pension scheme in question have power to determine the person to whom the sum, or any part of it, is to be paid, requiring them to pay the whole or part of that sum, when it becomes due, to the other party;

  (b) if the liable party has power to nominate the person to whom the sum, or any part of it, is to be paid, requiring the liable party to nominate the other party in respect of the whole or part of that sum;

  (c) in any other case, requiring the trustees or managers of the pension scheme in question to pay the whole or part of that sum, when it becomes due, to the other party instead of to the person to whom, apart from the order, it would be paid.

(4) Any payment by the trustees or managers under an order under subsection (2) or (3) above—

  (a) shall discharge so much of the trustees' or managers' liability to or in respect of the liable party as corresponds to the amount of the payment; and

  (b) shall be treated for all purposes as a payment made by the liable party in or towards the discharge of his liability under the capital sum order.

(5) Where the liability of the liable party under the capital sum order has been discharged in whole or in part, other than by a payment by the trustees or managers under an order under subsection (2) or (3) above, the court may, on an application by any person having an interest, recall any order under either of those subsections or vary the amount specified in such an order, as appears to the court appropriate in the circumstances.

(6) Where—

  (a) an order under subsection (2) or (3) above imposes any requirement on the trustees or managers of a pension scheme ("the first scheme") and the liable party acquires transfer credits under another scheme ("the new scheme") which are derived (directly or indirectly) from a transfer from the first scheme of all his accrued rights under that scheme; and

(b) the trustees or managers of the new scheme have been given notice in accordance with regulations under subsection (8) below,

the order shall have effect as if it had been made instead in respect of the trustees or managers of the new scheme; and in this subsection "transfer credits" has the same meaning as in the Pension Schemes Act 1993.

(7) Without prejudice to subsection (6) above, the court may, on an application by any person having an interest, vary an order under subsection (2) or (3) above by substituting for the trustees or managers specified in the order the trustees or managers of any other pension scheme under which any lump sum referred to in subsection (1) above is payable to the liable party or in respect of his death.

(8) The Secretary of State may by regulations—

(a) require notices to be given in respect of changes of circumstances relevant to orders under subsection (2) or (3) above;

(b) make provision for the recovery of the administrative expenses of complying with such orders from the liable party or the other party.

(9) Regulations under subsection (8) above shall be made by statutory instrument which shall be subject to annulment in pursuance of a resolution of either House of Parliament.

(10) Subsection (10) (other than the definition of "benefits under a pension scheme") and subsection (11) of section 10 of this Act shall apply for the purposes of this section as those subsections apply for the purposes of that section.

NOTE

1. Inserted by the Pensions Act 1995 (c. 26), s.167(3). Section 167(4) of the Pensions Act 1995 provides that "nothing in the provisions mentioned in section 166(5) [of the 1995 Act] applies to a court exercising its powers under section 8(orders for financial provision on divorce, etc.) or 12A (orders for payment of capital sum: pensions lump sums) of the 1985 Act in respect of any benefits under a pension scheme which fall within subsection (5)(b) of section 10 of that Act ("pension scheme" having the meaning given in subsection (10) of that section)."

DEFINITIONS

"the court": s.27(1).
"party to a marriage": s.27(1).
"matrimonial property": s.10(4).

GENERAL NOTE

This provides for what is generally known as an "earmarking order". It is proving extremely complex to apply in practice. Orders are being made in terms that pension trustees claim are unworkable. If pension interests form a large part of the matrimonial property and there is no compelling need for urgency in the ending of the marriage, waiting until the possibility of pension splitting becomes an option could be advisable. The Welfare Reform and Pensions Act 1999 sets out the framework for pension sharing. Detailed regulations are being finalised. An agreement for pension sharing could be set out in a separation agreement but would only become binding on the pension trustees or managers on intimation following decree of divorce. Since the regulations are being finalised it would be unwise to enter into an agreement at this stage that relied on pension sharing. Where an "earmarking order" is to be craved, the wording of the order should be checked with the pension trustees or managers before being submitted to court. The craves should be worded to show the order sought under this provision as a method of payment ancillary to a capital sum order. The capital sum order could then be enforced in other ways in the event of the "earmarking order" failing for one reason or another, or paying only part of the capital sum due (including interest). The beneficiary of the order must give notice to the pension trustees or managers of any change in his or her address within 14 days of moving.

Subs. (1)

The pension interests must form part of the matrimonial property and must include payment of a lump sum. One of the weaknesses of reliance on an "earmarking order" is that many schemes either do not pay out on death or only pay a small amount, insufficient to satisfy the capital sum order. Another weakness is that in some pension schemes there is an option to commute part or all of the lump sum which if exercised would defeat the earmarking order. At least one pension provider has indicated that it does not believe an earmarking order to be competent where the lump sum is only an option. While doubt has been cast on that view, it reinforces the pitfalls and the need for a "belt, braces and bit of a string approach" if contemplating an earmarking order.

Subs. (2)

Before seeking such an order it is important to find out as much as possible about the amount and timing of payment of the pension lump sum. In most cases there will be some possible variations depending on choices made by the one entitled to the pension or the possibility of death prior to retirement. The wording of the orders sought must be clear enough to allow the pension administrators to calculate exactly what is due, but flexible enough to admit the possibility of payment partially from the lump sum and partially from other assets.

Subs. (3)

Information about the liability of the pension fund, if any, to make payment in the event of death prior to retirement should be ascertained before any decision is made about the appropriateness of an "earmarking order". The possibility of insurance cover as a further security could be considered.

Subs. (5)

The "liable party" may be lucky on the lottery or inherit money after the making of the "earmarking order" and decide to make payment in part or full to their former spouse at an earlier point. Since interest will normally be running on the outstanding balance it could make sense to use other resources to make settlement. This provision allows variation of the order in those circumstances.

Subs. (6)

This highlights another concern about relying on such orders. Although provision is made for transfer there has to be some risk that through ambiguity or oversight the paperwork will not be properly completed and implementation fail.

S.I.s ISSUED UNDER SECTION

Divorce etc. (Pensions) (Scotland) Regulations S.I. 1996 No. 1901.
Divorce etc. (Pensions) (Scotland) Amendment Regulations S.I. 1997 No. 745.

Orders for periodical allowance

13.—(1) An order under section 8(2) of this Act for a periodical allowance may be made—

(a) on granting decree of divorce;

(b) within such period as the court on granting decree of divorce may specify; or

(c) after decree of divorce where—

    (i) no such order has been made previously;

    (ii) application for the order has been made after the date of decree; and

    (iii) since the date of decree there has been a change of circumstances.

(2) The court shall not make an order for a periodical allowance under section 8(2) of this Act unless—

(a) the order is justified by a principle set out in paragraph (c), (d) or (e) of section 9(1) of this Act; and

(b) it is satisfied that an order for payment of a capital sum or for transfer of property under that section would be inappropriate or insufficient to satisfy the requirements of the said section 8(2).

(3) An order under section 8(2) of this Act for a periodical allowance may be for a definite or an indefinite period or until the happening of a specified event.

(4) Where an order for a periodical allowance has been made under section 8(2) of this Act, and since the date of the order there has been a

material change of circumstances, the court shall, on an application by or on behalf of either party to the marriage or his executor, have power by subsequent order—

(a) to vary or recall the order for a periodical allowance;

(b) to backdate such variation or recall to the date of the application therefor or, on cause shown, to an earlier date;

(c) to convert the order into an order for payment of a capital sum or for a transfer of property.

[1] (4A) Without prejudice to the generality of subsection (4) above, the making of a maintenance assessment with respect to a child who has his home with a person to whom the periodical allowance is made (being a child to whom the person making the allowance has an obligation of aliment) is a material change of circumstances for the purposes of that subsection.

(5) The provisions of this Act shall apply to applications and orders under subsection (4) above as they apply to applications for periodical allowance and orders on such applications.

(6) Where the court backdates an order under subsection (4)(b) above, the court may order any sums paid by way of periodical allowance to be repaid.

(7) An order for a periodical allowance made under section 8(2) of this Act—

(a) shall, if subsisting at the death of the party making the payment, continue to operate against the party's estate, but without prejudice to the making of an order under subsection (4) above;

(b) shall cease to have effect on the remarriage or death of the party receiving payment, except in relation to any arrears due under it.

NOTE
1. Inserted by S.I. 1993 No. 660.

DEFINITIONS
"aliment": s.27(1).
"child": s.27(1).
"the court": s.27(1).
"decree of divorce": s.17(2).
"maintenance assessment": s.27(1).
"party to a marriage": s.27(1).
"property": s.27(1).

GENERAL NOTE
This should be read along with ss.8(2) and 9(1)(c), (d) and (e). Periodical allowance cannot be used to satisfy financial provision under s.9(1)(a) or (b). It is only competent in relation to s.9(1)(c), (d) or (e) when a capital payment would be inappropriate or insufficient. Since a payment of capital can be made by instalments in terms of s.12(3) it would be possible to seek capital by instalments rather than periodical allowance. Variation of instalment of capital can only be made in terms of s.12(4) to alter the method of payment, not the amount. It would therefore be attractive for a recipient to seek payment of capital by instalments rather than periodical allowance. Such an approach would seem at odds with the underlying purpose of the s.9(1)(c), (d) and (e) principles which are intended to allow provision for future circumstances, not to achieve an appropriate division of matrimonial assets under s.9(1)(a) and (b) which relate to the past. If capital is available at the time of the orders to make appropriate adjustment under s.9(1)(c), (d) or (e) then it would allow a "clean break" and may be the practical solution to problems such as housing needs. If there is no capital available then the payments will be coming from income and the wider provision for variation of periodical allowance in this section would be appropriate.

Subs. (1)
Usually if the court is satisfied that a periodical allowance is justified this will be on the basis of an existing need and existing resources and granted at the time of the divorce or at a subsequent proof or adjourned diet (*Mackin v. Mackin*, 1991 S.L.T.(Sh. Ct) 22). There have been circumstances which have led to a suspended award. In *Shipton v. Shipton*, 1992 S.C.L.R. 23 an award of periodical allowance was made for three years but suspended until the husband

obtained employment. Following the logic of that case, if a spouse had the need for financial provision for adjustment or because of hardship, could not obtain a capital payment on divorce and at that point the other spouse had no foreseeable prospects of paying periodical allowance and no such award was made, then an application under s.13(1)(c) could be made within three years of the divorce in the case of potential provision for adjustment and potentially at any stage in respect of hardship if the financial circumstances of the other spouse improved. It is, however, difficult to see how to establish the substantial dependence or that the divorce is the cause of serious financial hardship if at the time of divorce the potential payer is not in good financial health unless it were accepted that the divorce ended the possibility of resuming financial support which had been provided before (extending the decision in *Haugan v. Haugan,* 1996 S.L.T. 321 that the loss of the right to aliment on divorce would itself be a hardship brought about by the divorce rather than by the separation). It does seem to stretch the undoubted elasticity of the Act to contemplate such claims. If arrangements for the care of children were to change after divorce a claim based on s.9(1)(c) could become appropriate.

Such an action should be by way of initial writ and could follow a simplified procedure divorce, although it is particularly difficult to envisage how s.9(1)(c), (d) or (e) principles could be justified in such a case (see *Murray v. Murray,* 1990 S.C.L.R. 226).

Subs. (2)
Para. (b)

It is essential to have appropriate averments in relation to s.11(3), (4) or (5) considerations, pleas in law specifying whichever of the s.9(1)(c), (d) and (e) principles is founded on, and it must be established that a capital or transfer of property order is not an option (*Thirde v. Thirde,* 1987 S.C.L.R. 335). In *Mackin v. Mackin,* 1991 S.L.T.(Sh. Ct) 22 there was no averment that capital would be insufficient and so periodical allowance was refused.

Subs. (3)

Clearly there are infinite possible permutations but some examples are:

(a) *Definite period*

Dever v. Dever, 1988 S.C.L.R. 352. A 27-year-old wife lived with her husband for six years prior to the separation and at the time of divorce was on state benefits. She was awarded periodical allowance for a period of six months as she had shown the capacity to survive without her husband's help for 18 months since the separation. There were no children.

Petrie v. Petrie, 1988 S.C.L.R. 390. A wife aged 42 had cohabited for four years prior to the two-year period of cohabitation following marriage. It was considered that the whole period of cohabitation should be relevant to determine the wife's dependence, which was total. She had no qualifications for employment and was in receipt of state benefits. She had not claimed support following the separation because she thought her adultery would disentitle her from any support. Her husband who was disabled was dependent on income from invested capital. Periodical allowance was awarded for one year to enable the wife to seek employment. There was one child of the wife's previous marriage living with her.

Atkinson v. Atkinson, 1988 S.C.L.R. 396. In addition to a capital settlement the wife was awarded periodical allowance for three years from the date of decree. Although she was earning an income it was not sufficient considering the standard of life she enjoyed during the marriage.

Tyrrell v. Tyrrell, 1990 S.L.T. 406. The couple were married and lived together for 18 years. There were no children. The wife was alimented for seven years of separation. Periodical allowance was awarded for one year for adjustment although the wife was by then in part time employment.

(b) *Indefinite period*

Johnstone v. Johnstone, 1990 S.L.T.(Sh. Ct) 79. The wife aged 35 was unable to work because she suffered from epilepsy. There was one teenage child. The couple had been married and lived together for 13 years. The wife was awarded periodical allowance of 100 per month until her death or remarriage.

McKenzie v. McKenzie, 1991 S.L.T. 461. The couple were married and lived together for 16 years. There were no dependent children. Although the wife ran a small business she had very little income from it. She would be entitled to a small pension at 60 and was awarded a capital sum but it was recognised that she was likely to be short of money even then and periodical allowance was awarded indefinitely.

Haugan v. Haugan, 1996 S.L.T. 321. A 51-year-old wife who had been married and lived with her husband for 27 years. She had various health problems including mental health problems and a very restricted earning capacity. She was entitled to periodical allowance under this heading until her death or remarriage. The fact that she had not been receiving support during the separation did not preclude an award under s.9(1)(e)—it was the divorce not the separation which posed the potential hardship of the loss of the right to aliment.

(c) *The happening of a specified event*

Bell v. *Bell*, 1988 S.C.L.R. (Sh. Ct) 457. A 51-year-old wife received an award of periodical allowance until the husband then aged 53 retired at 60 (or her own earlier death or remarriage).

Subs. (4)

Material change of circumstances

Usually this will be established by a significant increase or decrease in income or a change of dependants. Someone paying periodical allowance might assume that if their former spouse started living with a new partner the obligation would cease automatically. That is not the case. The cohabitation would be a material change of circumstances. It would be a "very important fact and can be ... a deciding factor" but if the new partner is not providing support the periodical allowance may be allowed to remain in payment (*Kavanagh* v. *Kavanagh*, 1989 S.L.T. 134).

Material change of circumstances does not cover the situation where an original award is made on the basis of incorrect or incomplete information or on a hypothesis which subsequently proves incorrect (see *Stewart* v. *Stewart*, 1987 S.L.T. 246 (a pre-1985 Act case), *Walker* v. *Walker*, 1995 S.L.T. 375, and *Bye* v. *Bye*, 1999 G.W.D. 33–1591).

Pre-1985 provisions. Mitchell v. *Mitchell*, 1993 S.L.T. 419. It was held to be competent to vary both the level and duration of periodical allowance.

Para. (a)

What should be the starting point in considering what variation (if any) would be appropriate where there has been a material change of circumstances? In *Sutherland* v. *Sutherland*, 1988 S.C.L.R. 346 the sheriff decided not to take the previous order as the starting point but the Inner House decision in *Macpherson* v. *Macpherson*, 1989 S.L.T. 231 took an opposite view. The First Division decision of *Johnsen* v. *Johnsen*, 1995 G.W.D. 10–524 (dealing with aliment) set out that the material change circumstances must first be established, then a comparison made between the financial circumstances at the time of the making of award and at the date of variation.

Periodical allowance awarded under s.9(1)(d) could not be varied to continue beyond three years from the granting of divorce.

Para. (b)

The court has discretion in whether or not to order backdating. In *Law* v. *Law*, 1991 G.W.D. 11–664 it was not ordered.

Backdating cannot be ordered when a variation of periodical allowance was awarded prior to the Acts coming into force (*Wilson* v. *Wilson*, 1992 S.L.T. 664).

Para. (c)

Subsection (7)(a) provides that the death of the payer does not bring the obligation to an end although it leaves open the possibility of an executor seeking variation. Converting an order under this provision may be appropriate where the estate is quite substantial.

There could be other circumstances in which conversion might be appropriate. If a payer of periodical allowance, particularly an allowance awarded under s.9(1)(e), were to inherit money after the divorce it might make sense to attempt to capitalise the award. The payer would then lose the possibility of an improvement in the recipient's circumstances diminishing or eliding the obligation. The dearth of cases exploring this possibility may reflect what a small part ongoing spousal support plays in financial provision on divorce.

Subs. (4A)

In *Stokes* v. *Stokes*, 1999 S.C.L.R. 327 the sheriff principal upheld a decision declining to reduce spousal aliment payable *ad interim* by exactly the amount of a subsequent Child Support Agency maintenance assessment and instead, carried out a general reassessment. Although it does not deal with periodical allowance this case may be of some relevance.

Incidental orders

14.—(1) Subject to subsection (3) below, an incidental order may be made under section 8(2) of this Act before, on or after the granting or refusal of decree of divorce.

(2) In this Act, "an incidental order" means one or more of the following orders—

(a) an order for the sale of property;

(b) an order for the valuation of property;

(c) an order determining any dispute between the parties to the marriage as to their respective property rights by means of a declarator thereof or otherwise;

(d) an order regulating the occupation of the matrimonial home or the use of furniture and plenishings therein or excluding either party to the marriage from such occupation;

(e) an order regulating liability, as between the parties, for outgoings in respect of the matrimonial home or furniture or plenishings therein;

(f) an order that security shall be given for any financial provision;

(g) an order that payments shall be made or property transferred to any curator bonis or trustee or other person for the benefit of the party to the marriage by whom or on whose behalf application has been made under section 8(1) of this Act for an incidental order;

(h) an order setting aside or varying any term in an antenuptial or postnuptial marriage settlement;

(j) an order as to the date from which any interest on any amount awarded shall run;

(k) any ancillary order which is expedient to give effect to the principles set out in section 9 of this Act or to any order made under section 8(2) of this Act.

(3) An incidental order referred to in subsection (2)(d) or (e) above may be made only on or after the granting of decree of divorce.

(4) An incidental order may be varied or recalled by subsequent order on cause shown.

(5) So long as an incidental order granting a party to a marriage the right to occupy a matrimonial home or the right to use furniture and plenishings therein remains in force then—

(a) section 2(1), (2), (5)(a) and (9) of the Matrimonial Homes (Family Protection) (Scotland) Act 1981 (which confer certain general powers of management on a spouse in relation to a matrimonial home), and

[1] (b) subject to section 15(3) of this Act, section 12 of the said Act of 1981 and section 41 of the Bankruptcy (Scotland) Act 1985 (which protect the occupancy rights of a spouse against arrangements intended to defeat them),

shall, except to the extent that the order otherwise provides, apply in relation to the order—

(i) as if that party were a non-entitled spouse and the other party were an entitled spouse within the meaning of section 1(1) or 6(2) of the said Act of 1981 as the case may require;

(ii) as if the right to occupy a matrimonial home under that order were "occupancy rights" within the meaning of the said Act of 1981; and

(iii) with any other necessary modifications; and

subject to section 15(3) of this Act, section 11 of the said Act of 1981 (protection of spouse in relation to furniture and plenishings) shall apply in relation to the order as if that party were a spouse within the meaning of the said section 11 and the order were an order under section 3(3) or (4) of the said Act of 1981.

(6) In subsection (2)(h) above, "settlement" includes a settlement by way of a policy of assurance to which section 2 of the Married Women's Policies of Assurance (Scotland) Act 1880 relates.

(7) Notwithstanding subsection (1) above, the Court of Session may by Act of Sederunt make rules restricting the categories of incidental order which may be made under section 8(2) of this Act before the granting of decree of divorce.

NOTE

1. As amended by the Bankruptcy (Scotland) Act 1985 (c. 66), Sched. 7, para. 23.

DEFINITIONS
   "the court": s.27(1).
   "decree of divorce": s.17(2).
   "matrimonial home": s.27(1).
   "parties to the marriage": s.27(1).
   "settlement": s.14(5).

GENERAL NOTE
   These are orders incidental to financial provision and, in terms of s.8(2), must be justified by the s.9 principles, reasonable having regard to the resources of the parties and within the parameters of ss.12–15.
   Orders for the sale of property (subs. (2), para. (a)) and in relation to interest (subs. (2), para. (j)) have been the most frequently requested. Dealing with insurance policies has posed problems. Although an order can be sought transferring the interest in a policy from one spouse to the other, para. (k) is unlikely to confer sufficient power to allow the sheriff clerk to sign the deed of assignation if the defender proves to be recalcitrant or absent. Section 5A of the Sheriff Courts (Scotland) Act 1907 confers on the sheriff the power to direct the sheriff clerk to sign a deed relating to heritable property. This power can be requested where a transfer or sale of heritable property is craved and it is anticipated or established that the defender cannot be found or will not co-operate with a signature. The 1999 Consultation Paper explores the possibility of s.5A being amended to allow the sheriff to direct the sheriff clerk to execute deeds relating to moveable as well as heritable property.

Subs. (2)
Para. (a)
   It can be very helpful for all the legal steps to be covered within one action. Where the overall financial provision means that one person should receive more than one-half of the value of the matrimonial home the need for such an order is quite clear. If the outcome leaves a jointly owned matrimonial home still in joint names it is true that after divorce an action of division and sale would be relatively straightforward. However, it would be daunting for anyone to contemplate further proceedings. In *Jacques v. Jacques*, 1995 S.L.T. 963 (aff'd) and 1997 S.L.T. 459 an order for sale and equal division of the proceeds of a jointly owned property, allowed on appeal, was affirmed.
   The pleadings must be very precise and cover adequately the mechanics of sale to allow an appropriate order to be made (see "Division and sale of family homes", 1999 Fam.L.B. 37–6).
Para. (b)
   Any such request should be very precise in detailing who should carry out the valuation. The provision was considered in *Demarco v. Demarco*, 1990 S.C.L.R. 635 where it was seen as being restricted to property belonging to one of the couple. With some types of property it may be more appropriate to use the motion and specification procedure to obtain the relevant information to allow a valuation to be carried out. In the case of business interests or pension interests where the CETV may not reflect the relevant value some privacy might be preferable in obtaining the valuation!
Para. (d)
   This is not a widely used provision in litigation although rather more so in negotiation. If a matrimonial home cannot be transferred at the time of divorce there are two disadvantages to leaving it jointly owned or in the ownership of the party not living there. One is that the party living in the property may feel rather beholden to or controlled by the other. Another is the difficulty the party not living in the property would have in purchasing alternative accommodation if, as is usually the case, there is a secured loan over the former matrimonial home. It could however allow occupation to enable one parent to remain with the children in the family home for long enough to improve that parent's chance of securing an income which would allow the other parent to be released from the secured loan. The s.9 principles would need to justify any such order.
   Subs. (5) provides some powers of management and protection but care needs to be taken to guard against the possibility of sale during the period of occupancy.
Para. (e)
   This provision could be used in conjunction with an occupancy order or to cover a period up until the transfer of a property as in *McCormick v. McCormick*, 1991 G.W.D. 35–2078.
Para. (f)
   Any financial provision. This was considered unlikely to be wide enough to include providing security for an order for educational expenses in *Macdonald v. Macdonald*, 1995 S.L.T. 72. An

incidental order can be granted for a standard security to be granted over the former matrimonial home to secure payment of the capital sum payable from the sale proceeds (*Murley v. Murley*, 1995 S.C.L.R. 1138 and *Collins v. Collins*, 1997 Fam.L.R. 50).

Para. (h)

Section 9 principles and s.15(3) would have to be taken into account.

Para. (j)

This could be used to correct an imbalance that would otherwise occur because of a delay between the relevant date and date of the order where one person had been enjoying the use or possession of matrimonial property (*Geddes v. Geddes*, 1993 S.L.T. 494). In *Welsh v. Welsh*, 1994 S.L.T. 828 the title to the former matrimonial home was transferred to the husband. However, an award of interest was made from the date of separation on the element of capital representing the wife's share of equity in the matrimonial home to recognise the husband's economic advantage in living in the house and the corresponding disadvantage to the wife (although that approach was not taken in *Livie v. Livie*, 1999 G.W.D. 34–1639). If the 1999 Discussion Paper results in the transfers of property using the value at date of transfer rather than relevant date this provision may be needed less for that purpose. It would still be relevant to award interest on a deferred payment of capital even if the capital were based on the value of pension interests as in *Gulline v. Gulline*, 1992 S.L.T. 71.

In *Bolton v. Bolton*, 1995 G.W.D. 14–799 interest on a capital sum was fixed from a date subsequent to the date of separation but over two years prior to the order reflecting the earliest date assets on which the award were based could have been realised. It was recognised in that case that judicial interest is generally above the market rates. Various rates of interest have been used on deferred payments. If the period of the deferment is extensive a fluctuating rate such as 1 per cent below a specified bank's base lending rate might be appropriate in some circumstances. Factors to consider could include the nature of the asset on which the award is based and the impact on the party denied the use of the capital.

Rights of third parties

15.—(1) The court shall not make an order under section 8(2) of this Act for the transfer of property if the consent of a third party which is necessary under any obligation, enactment or rule of law has not been obtained.

(2) The court shall not make an order under section 8(2) of this Act for the transfer of property subject to security without the consent of the creditor unless he has been given an opportunity of being heard by the court.

(3) Neither an incidental order, nor any rights conferred by such an order, shall prejudice any rights of any third party insofar as those rights existed immediately before the making of the order.

DEFINITIONS
"the court": s.27(1).
"incidental order": s.14(2).
"property": s.27(1).

GENERAL NOTE

Subss (1) and (2)

The distinction between the two subsections is that where s.15(1) applies and there is a legal right to withhold consent such a right cannot be overridden by the court, but where s.15(2) applies and there is no legal right to withhold consent an opportunity must be given for the security holders, views to be heard and taken into account (*MacNaught v. MacNaught*, 1997 S.L.T. 60). Most securities will specify that the lender's consent must be given to any transfer. If so, evidence of that consent should be produced.

Subs. (3)

Thus an occupancy order granted under s.14(2)(d) would not override the rights of a heritable creditor.

Agreements on financial provision

16.—(1) Where the parties to a marriage have entered into an agreement as to financial provision to be made on divorce, the court may make an order setting aside or varying—

(a) any term of the agreement relating to a periodical allowance where the agreement expressly provides for the subsequent setting aside or variation by the court of that term; or

(b) the agreement or any term of it where the agreement was not fair and reasonable at the time it was entered into.

(2) The court may make an order—

(a) under subsection (1)(a) above at any time after granting decree of divorce; and

(b) under subsection (1)(b) above on granting decree of divorce or within such time thereafter as the court may specify on granting decree of divorce.

[1] (3) Without prejudice to subsections (1) and (2) above, where the parties to a marriage have entered into an agreement as to financial provision to be made on divorce and—

(a) the estate of the party by whom any periodical allowance is payable under the agreement has, since the date when the agreement was entered into, been sequestrated, the award of sequestration has not been recalled and the party has not been discharged;

(b) an analogous remedy within the meaning of section 10(5) of the Bankruptcy (Scotland) Act 1985 has, since that date, come into force and remains in force in respect of that party's estate;

(c) that party's estate is being administered by a trustee acting under a voluntary trust deed granted since that date by the party for the benefit of his creditors generally or is subject to an analogous arrangement; or

(d) by virtue of the making of a maintenance assessment, child support maintenance has become payable by either party to the agreement with respect to a child to whom or for whose benefit periodical allowance is paid under that agreement,

the court may, on or at any time after granting decree of divorce, make an order setting aside or varying any term of the agreement relating to the periodical allowance.

(4) Any term of an agreement purporting to exclude the right to apply for an order under subsection (1)(b) or (3) above shall be void.

(5) In this section, "agreement" means an agreement entered into before or after the commencement of this Act.

NOTE
1. As amended by S.I. 1993 No. 660.

DEFINITIONS
"agreement": s.16(5).
"child": s.27(1).
"child support maintenance": s.27(1).
"the court": s.27(1).
"maintenance assessment": s.27(1).
"parties to a marriage": s.27(1).

GENERAL NOTE
If parties choose to enter into a written agreement dealing with all the financial aspects of their separation it is important for them to be aware that there can be some circumstances in which that agreement could be reopened. It is also important to try to minimise the likelihood that such challenge would be probable or successful. From the 1997 Research two aspects seem crucial. One aspect is for the legal advisers to have adequate "people" skills. The other is for legal advisers to have adequate legal knowledge and drafting skills. Parties need and want to be given full information about the legal framework and the options open to them. This should be reinforced by the matrimonial assets and liabilities being clearly set out in the separation

agreement. If that is done it will be clear what was taken into account. It makes it more likely that gaps in disclosure would be identified. If full disclosure is made and both parties are aware of and able to grasp their legal rights, challenge in the future is unlikely to be successful even if the division in the agreement was very unequal. This makes it extremely important to encourage clients to do their own "reality testing" about how they might feel about the agreement on hindsight. Using "what if" questions can be very helpful. If the provision would still be acceptable should the spouse quickly acquire a new partner to share the fruits or after thinking hard about the likely impact on the post-agreement standard of living it is less likely that the terms will be regretted.

Subs. (1)
Para. (a)
In a separation agreement spousal support before divorce should be described as aliment and after divorce as periodical allowance, and a provision for potential variation by the court included.
Drummond v. Drummond, 1996 S.L.T. 386. A separation agreement included provision for "aliment" but no provision for variation of its terms. After the parties divorced it could not be varied either under s.16(1)(a) because there was no express power to do so or under s.7(2) because there was no obligation to aliment after divorce.
Ellerby v. Ellerby, 1991 S.C.L.R. 608. The court had no power to vary a agreement that did state that it was "subject to variation" but without stating how any such variation would be achieved.
This provision does not affect other grounds of challenge such as error, fraud, force and fear (but should offer a less stringent test—*McAfee v. McAfee,* 1990 S.C.L.R. 805 at p. 808c) and it cannot be excluded by contract (s.4).
Para. (b)
The principles to be taken into account were set out in detail in *Gillon v. Gillon (No. 3),* 1995 S.L.T. 678: (1) both fairness and reasonableness are to be considered; (2) all of the relevant circumstances prevailing are to be examined including the nature and quality of any legal advice; (3) unfair advantage taken by one party of the other may have "a cogent bearing"; (4) the court should "not be unduly ready to overturn agreements validly entered into"; (5) the fact of even very unequal division is not in itself evidence of unfairness and unreasonableness. The withholding of relevant information is a relevant factor (*Gillon v. Gillon, (No. 1),* 1994 S.L.T. 978 at p. 983).
Variation Granted
Worth v. Worth, 1994 S.L.T.(Sh.Ct) 54. Terms arrived at by the couple were recorded in a minute of agreement, only one solicitor was involved (as an "honest broker") and the parties were unaware that pension rights could be looked on as property.
Short v. Short, 1994 G.W.D. 21–1300. The wife was suffering from reactive depression to the extent of having a nervous breakdown following the separation, no provision was made for periodical allowance or capital sum and no enquiries had been made into the husband's salary or value of his pension. The wife was advised by her solicitor to accept the agreement.
Variation Refused
Gillon v. Gillon (No. 3), 1995 S.L.T. 678. The settlement was unequal but accorded with the party's wishes at the time after full discussion and with appropriate knowledge.
In *Inglis v. Inglis,* 1999 S.L.T. (Sh.Ct) 59 variation was not allowed even although the settlement did not take into account the value of the husband's pension interests and the wife did not take independent legal advice as she was told of her potential claim and advised to get legal advice.
Joint Minute or Tender
An agreement recorded in a joint minute or in a tender and minute of acceptance could fall within this subsection but the provisions must be invoked before the minute is implemented.
Jongejan v. Jongejan, 1993 S.L.T. 595 (joint minute) and *Young v. Young (No. 2),* 1991 S.L.T. 869 (tender) are other cases worth considering.
See also Junor, G., "Challenging Separation Agreements", 1998 S.L.T. 185.

Financial provision on declarator of nullity of marriage

17.—(1) Subject to the following provisions of this section, the provisions of this Act shall apply to actions for declarator of nullity of marriage as they apply to actions for divorce; and in this Act, unless the context otherwise requires, "action for divorce" includes an action for declarator of nullity of marriage and, in relation to such an action, "decree" and "divorce" shall be construed accordingly.

(2) In an action for declarator of nullity of marriage, it shall be competent for either party to claim interim aliment under section 6(1) of this Act notwithstanding that he denies the existence of the marriage.

(3) Any rule of law by virtue of which either party to an action for declarator of nullity of marriage may require restitution of property upon the granting of such declarator shall cease to have effect.

DEFINITION
    "marriage": s.27(1).

Supplemental

Orders relating to avoidance transactions

18.—(1) Where a claim has been made (whether before or after the commencement of this Act), being—
    (a) an action for aliment,
    (b) a claim for an order for financial provision, or
    (c) an application for variation or recall of a decree in such an action or of an order for financial provision,
the party making the claim may, not later than one year from the date of the disposal of the claim, apply to the court for an order—
    (i) setting aside or varying any transfer of, or transaction involving, property effected by the other party not more than five years before the date of the making of the claim; or
    (ii) interdicting the other party from effecting any such transfer or transaction.

(2) Subject to subsection (3) below, on an application under subsection (1) above for an order the court may, if it is satisfied that the transfer or transaction had the effect of, or is likely to have the effect of, defeating in whole or in part any claim referred to in subsection (1) above, make the order applied for or such other order as it thinks fit.

(3) An order under subsection (2) above shall not prejudice any rights of a third party in or to the property where that third party—
    (a) has in good faith acquired the property or any of it or any rights in relation to it for value; or
    (b) derives title to such property or rights from any person who has done so.

(4) Where the court makes an order under subsection (2) above, it may include in the order such terms and conditions as it thinks fit and may make any ancillary order which it considers expedient to ensure that the order is effective.

DEFINITIONS
    "action for aliment": ss.2(3) and 27(1).
    "the court": s.27(1).
    "decree": s.27(1).
    "order for financial provision": ss.8(3) and 27(1).

GENERAL NOTE
    Working out whether disclosure or a disposal is being made can be a difficult and anxious aspect of negotiations. The anti-avoidance provisions offer a measure of protection. Adequate information is required to substantiate the need for them in the written pleadings or minute in the process post divorce. It is not essential to prove intention to defeat a claim, the test is objective. If an unnecessary order is sought any co-operation in negotiations is likely to evaporate. If not sought when necessary the consequences could be very serious.

Subs. (1)
    The period of five years is to cover the maximum time under the Divorce (Scotland) Act 1976 which could elapse between separation and the possibility of divorce. The 1999 Consultation

Paper explores the option of establishing irretrievable breakdown by two rather than five years' separation without consent. If that option were taken it would be logical to reduce the scope of this provision.

The definition of "court" in s.27(1) makes it appear that the sheriff court can deal with what might otherwise have been interpreted as effectively an action of reduction competent only in the Court of Session (see *Hernandez-Cimorra v. Hernandez-Cimorra*, 1992 S.C.L.R. 611). The provision could cover setting aside a gift of money and has been used to reduce a decree (*Tahir v. Tahir (No. 2)*, 1995 S.L.T. 451).

The existing remedies for breach of interdict apply. If an interdict is knowingly breached a period of imprisonment would not be excessive.

Robertson v. Robertson, 1996 G.W.D. 3–167. An interdict against disposal was granted but disobeyed and a period of imprisonment imposed in consequence although an appeal against the disposal continued to allow the possibility of at least part payment.

Subs. (3)

For consideration of the impact of mandates see *Hernandez-Cimorra v. Hernandez-Cimorra*, 1992 S.C.L.R. 611.

If a third party might be affected by such an order he or she should be given the opportunity of being heard (*Harris v. Harris*, 1988 S.L.T. 101).

For consideration of similar provisions in the Divorce (Scotland) Act 1976 see *Leslie v. Leslie*, 1987 S.L.T. 232.

Inhibition and arrestment

19.—(1) Where a claim has been made, being—

(a) an action for aliment, or

(b) a claim for an order for financial provision,

the court shall have power, on cause shown, to grant warrant for inhibition or warrant for arrestment on the dependence of the action in which the claim is made and, if it thinks fit, to limit the inhibition to any particular property or to limit the arrestment to any particular property or to funds not exceeding a specified value.

(2) In subsection (1) above, "the court" means the Court of Session in relation to a warrant for inhibition and the Court of Session or the sheriff, as the case may require, in relation to a warrant for arrestment on the dependence.

(3) This section is without prejudice to section 1 of the Law Reform (Miscellaneous Provisions) (Scotland) Act 1966 (wages, pensions, etc., to be exempt from arrestment on the dependence of an action).

DEFINITIONS
"action for aliment": ss.2(3) and 27(1).
"order for financial provision": ss.8(3) and 27(1).

GENERAL NOTE

Subs. (1)
Para. (b)
Cause should be shown before the granting of an inhibition.

Thom v. Thom, 1990 S.C.L.R. 800. An inhibition granted without cause having been shown was recalled, the sale has allowed to proceed but consignation of the proceeds ordered. The test of showing cause was intended to make inhibition and arrestment easier to obtain than before, when special circumstances had to be shown, and reduce the need for interdict.

Matheson v. Matheson, 1994 G.W.D. 22–1362. An example of an arrestment which was later recalled as interfering with the husband's legitimate business operations and not of any legitimate advantage to the wife.

Provision of details of resources

20. In an action—

(a) for aliment;

(b) which includes a claim for an order for financial provision; or

    (c) which includes a claim for interim aliment,
the court may order either party to provide details of his resources or those
relating to a child or incapax on whose behalf he is acting.

DEFINITIONS
    "action": s.27(1).
    "action for aliment": ss.2(3) and 27(1).
    "the court": s.27(1).
    "order for financial provision": ss.8(3) and 27(1).

GENERAL NOTE
    Obtaining full financial information can still be a daunting task. Motion and specification
procedure is likely to be necessary to obtain complete particulars if confronted with non-
disclosure. Any attempt to force disclosure where concealment may be happening requires
extensive knowledge which may not always be available. It would seem helpful to put the onus
of disclosure on the parties at the earliest stage possible where financial orders are in issue.
    As s.27(1) defines "resources" as "present and foreseeable resources" this provision is of
limited assistance in obtaining information in relation to the value of the matrimonial property
at the relevant date.
    It is unnecessary to have averments that resources are being concealed (*Lawrence v.
Lawrence*, 1992 S.C.L.R. 199).
    If a party ordered to provide details of his resources fails to do so he will be in contempt.
However the court has no power to conduct an inquiry into the extent of the disclosure. Details,
not valuations, are to be provided (*Nelson v. Nelson*, 1993 S.C.L.R. 149).
    Stewart v. Callaghan, 1995 G.W.D. 29–1543. This deals with consideration of how to obtain
evidence from other jurisdictions.

Award of aliment or custody where divorce or separation refused

    [1] **21.** A court which refuses a decree of divorce or separation shall not, by
virtue of such refusal, be prevented from making an order for aliment.

NOTE
    1.   As amended by the Children (Scotland) Act 1995 (c. 36), s.105(5) and Sched. 5.

DEFINITIONS
    "the court": s.27(1).
    "decree of divorce": s.17(2).

Expenses of action

    22. The expenses incurred by a party to a marriage in pursuing or
defending—
    (a) an action for aliment brought by either party to the marriage on his
        own behalf against the other party;
    (b) an action for divorce, separation, declarator of marriage or
        declarator of nullity of marriage;
    (c) an application made after the commencement of this Act for
        variation or recall of a decree of aliment or an order for financial
        provision in an action brought before or after the commencement of
        this Act,
shall not be regarded as necessaries for which the other party to the
marriage is liable.

DEFINITIONS
    "action for aliment": ss.2(3) and 27(1).
    "order for financial provision": ss.8(3) and 27(1).

GENERAL NOTE
    This provision ended the husband's previous liability for expenses. It has not been replaced
with the principle that expenses follow success in the same way as other civil litigation. Family
actions often involve many issues with no clear "winner".

"No fault" grounds. Craigie v. Craigie, 1979 S.L.T.(Notes) 60. This case considered various issues expenses including comments that the normal rule in an undefended action based on five years' separation is no award of expenses.

Since consent would be withheld in an action based on the two-year separation period if it had an unwelcome crave for expenses, the rule is effectively the same there.

Conduct of case. Whittome v. Whittome (No. 2), 1994 S.L.T. 130. The wife's expenses were awarded against the husband as her conduct of the litigation was generally reasonable and she had been mainly successful. It was observed that an additional fee would have been refused.

Adams v. Adams (No. 2) 1997 S.L.T. 150 (and see "An Expensive Warning", 1995 Fam.L.B. 16–2) where an award of the expenses of the proof (though not the earlier procedure) was made to a husband where the wife failed on the two issues of principle which had occasioned the proof. Helpful guidance was provided. "In exercising its discretion as to expenses, the court may take into account such matters as the reasonableness of the parties' claims, the extent to which they have co-operated in disclosing, and agreeing on, the value of their respective assets, the offers they have made to settle, the extent to which proof could have been avoided, and of course the final outcome".

De Winton v. De Winton, 1997 S.L.T. 1118. Expenses were divided but it was made clear there was no "normal rule" to that effect. The wife was awarded much less than she asked for but more than was offered. The husband had legal aid.

Cullen v. Cullen, 1997 G.W.D. 2–59. Even though he was in receipt of legal aid the husband was found liable to nearly half the wife's expenses because of his conduct.

General. Gribb v. Gribb, 1993 S.L.T. 178. This was an action raised in the Court of Session. The husband was successful in having the case remitted to the sheriff court on the basis of expense. The wife's desire to avoid publicity was outweighed by the expense of defending an action in the Court of Session.

Buchanan v. Buchanan, 1998 G.W.D. 18–929. The case settled prior to proof. The question of expenses had not been resolved, however, and the wife sought expenses because of the husband's conduct of the case. No expenses were found due to or by either party as there was no agreement as to the factual background.

Bremner v. Bremner, 1998 S.L.T. 844. A solicitor's firm was found personally liable in expenses because of a failure to intimate to the paramour as the case was under the old rules with no discretion on that point!

Actions for aliment of small amounts

23. *[Substitutes new s.3 of the Sheriff Courts (Civil Jurisdiction and Procedure) (Scotland) Act 1963.]*

GENERAL NOTE

An action for aliment alone may be raised as a summary cause action in the sheriff court if the amount requested is below the stipulated amount (currently 70 per week in respect of a spouse and 35 per week in respect of a child). These amounts can be varied by the Lord Advocate by Statutory Instrument.

Matrimonial property, etc.

Marriage not to affect property rights or legal capacity

24.—(1) Subject to the provisions of any enactment (including this Act), marriage shall not of itself affect—

(a) the respective rights of the parties to the marriage in relation to their property;

(b) the legal capacity of the parties to the marriage.

(2) Nothing in subsection (1) above affects the law of succession.

DEFINITION

"parties to the marriage": s.27(1).

GENERAL NOTE

This consolidated the removal of legal restrictions in relation to the property and of contractual rights of married women which began with the Conjugal Rights (Scotland) Amendment Act 1861.

EDINBURGH UNIVERSITY LIBRARY WITHDRAWN

Presumption of equal shares in household goods

25.—(1) If any question arises (whether during or after a marriage) as to the respective rights of ownership of the parties to a marriage in any household goods obtained in prospect of or during the marriage other than by gift or succession from a third party, it shall be presumed, unless the contrary is proved, that each has a right to an equal share in the goods in question.

(2) For the purposes of subsection (1) above, the contrary shall not be treated as proved by reason only that while the parties were married and living together the goods in question were purchased from a third party by either party alone or by both in unequal shares.

(3) In this section "household goods" means any goods (including decorative or ornamental goods) kept or used at any time during the marriage in any matrimonial home for the joint domestic purposes of the parties to the marriage, other than—

(a) money or securities;
(b) any motor car, caravan or other road vehicle;
(c) any domestic animal.

DEFINITIONS
"caravan": s.27(1).
"household goods": s.25(3).
"matrimonial home": s.27(1).
"parties to a marriage": s.27(1).

GENERAL NOTE
The wording of s.1 excludes wedding presents from the presumption of joint ownership when taken with s.10(4)(a). Neither will such items be treated as matrimonial property. The question of ownership revolves round the intention of the donor and delivery (see *McDonald v. McDonald*, 1953 S.L.T.(Sh. Ct) 36) but note that reference to a "practical rule" of regarding as the owner of the present the spouse from whose friends or relatives the gift was received was described by Dr Clive as "although rather appealing—anthropologically ... unsupported by principle or authority" (*Husband and Wife* (4th ed.), p. 228 N 95).

Presumption of equal shares in money and property derived from housekeeping allowance

26. If any question arises (whether during or after a marriage) as to the right of a party to a marriage to money derived from any allowance made by either party for their joint household expenses or for similar purposes, or to any property acquired out of such money, the money or property shall, in the absence of any agreement between them to the contrary, be treated as belonging to each party in equal shares.

DEFINITION
"party to a marriage": s.27(1).

GENERAL NOTE
Derived from. If one spouse has a win on the lottery funded out of the housekeeping money provided by the other, *Pyatt v. Pyatt*, 1966 S.L.T.(Notes) 73 suggests that the prize money would be treated as joint. It would presumably be included as matrimonial property in any event should the impact of the win drive the couple apart, although an attempt to argue a case for unequal sharing might loom.

General

Interpretation

27.—(1) In this Act, unless the context otherwise requires—
"action" means an action brought after the commencement of this Act;

"action for aliment" has the meaning assigned to it by section 2(3) of this Act;

"aliment" does not include aliment *pendente lite* or interim aliment under section 6 of this Act;

"caravan" means a caravan which is mobile or affixed to the land;

[1] "child" includes a child whether or not his parents have ever been married to one another, and any reference to the child of a marriage (whether or not subsisting) includes a child (other than a child who has been boarded out with the parties, or one of them, by a local or other public authority or a voluntary organisation) who has been accepted by the parties as a child of the family;

[2] "child support maintenance" has the meaning assigned to it by section 3(6) of the Child Support Act 1991;

"the court" means the Court of Session or the sheriff, as the case may require;

"decree" in an action for aliment includes an order of the court awarding aliment;

"family" includes a one-parent family;

"incidental order" has the meaning assigned to it by section 14(2) of this Act;

[2] "maintenance assessment" has the meaning assigned to it by section 54 of the Child Support Act 1991;

"marriage", in relation to an action for declarator of nullity of marriage, means purported marriage;

[3] "matrimonial home" has the meaning assigned to it by section 22 of the Matrimonial Homes (Family Protection) (Scotland) Act 1981 as amended by section 13(10) of the Law Reform (Miscellaneous Provisions) (Scotland) Act 1985;

"needs" means present and foreseeable needs;

"obligation of aliment" shall be construed in accordance with section 1(2) of this Act;

"order for financial provision" means an order under section 8(2) of this Act and, in sections 18(1) and 22(c) of this Act, also includes an order under section 5(2) of the Divorce (Scotland) Act 1976;

"party to a marriage" and "party to the marriage" include a party to a marriage which has been terminated or annulled;

"property" in sections 8, 12, 13 and 15 of this Act does not include a tenancy transferable under section 13 of the Matrimonial Homes (Family Protection) (Scotland) Act 1981;

"resources" means present and foreseeable resources;

"voluntary organisation" means a body, other than a local or other public authority, the activities of which are not carried on for profit.

(2) For the purposes of this Act, the parties to a marriage shall be held to cohabit with one another only when they are in fact living together as man and wife.

NOTES

1. As amended by the Law Reform (Parent and Child) (Scotland) Act 1986 (c. 9), Sched. 1, para. 21.
2. Inserted by S.I. 1993 No. 660.
3. As amended by the Law Reform (Miscellaneous Provisions) (Scotland) Act 1985 (c. 73), Sched. 2, para. 31.

Amendments, repeals and savings

28.—(1) The enactments specified in Schedule 1 to this Act shall have effect subject to the amendments set out therein.

(2) The enactments specified in columns 1 and 2 of Schedule 2 to this Act are repealed to the extent specified in column 3 of that Schedule.

(3) Nothing in subsection (2) above shall affect the operation of section 5 (orders for financial provision) of the Divorce (Scotland) Act 1976 in relation to an action for divorce brought before the commencement of this Act; but in the continued operation of that section the powers of the court—
  (a) to make an order for payment of periodical allowance under subsection (2) thereof; and
  (b) to vary such an order under subsection (4) thereof,
shall include power to make such an order for a definite or an indefinite period or until the happening of a specified event.

DEFINITION
"the court": s.27(1).

GENERAL NOTE
Although *Mitchell v. Mitchell*, 1993 S.L.T. 419, confirmed the competence of varying both the level and duration of pre-1985 Act periodical allowance, *Gray v. Gray*,1999 Fam.L.R. 135, emphasised that the restrictions imposed by s.13(2) of this Act have no application. Variation is to be considered in light of the means of the parties and the whole circumstances of the case.

Citation, commencement and extent

29.—(1) This Act may be cited as the Family Law (Scotland) Act 1985.
¹ (2) This Act shall come into operation on such day as the Secretary of State may appoint by order made by statutory instrument, and different days may be appointed for different purposes.
(3) An order under subsection (2) above may contain such transitional provisions and savings as appear to the Secretary of State necessary or expedient in connection with the provisions brought into force (whether wholly or partly) by the order.
(4) So much of section 28 of, and Schedule 1 to, this Act as affects the operation of the Maintenance Orders Act 1950 and the Maintenance Orders (Reciprocal Enforcement) Act 1972 shall extend to England and Wales and to Northern Ireland as well as to Scotland, but save as aforesaid this Act shall extend to Scotland only.

SCHEDULES

Section 28(1)   SCHEDULE 1

MINOR AND CONSEQUENTIAL AMENDMENTS

The Sheriff Courts (Scotland) Act 1907 (c. 51)

1. In section 5 of the Sheriff Courts (Scotland) Act 1907 (jurisdiction), for subsection (2) there shall be substituted the following subsection—
    "(2) Actions for aliment or separation (other than any action mentioned in subsection (2A) below) and actions for regulating the custody of children:".

The Guardianship of Infants Act 1925 (c. 45)

2. In section 3(3) of the Guardianship of Infants Act 1925 (orders for custody and access not enforceable while parents living together), for the words from the beginning to the word accrue there shall be substituted the words "No such order for custody or education shall be enforceable".

The Maintenance Orders Act 1950 (c. 37)

3. In section 16(2)(b)(i) of the Maintenance Orders Act 1950 (enforcement of maintenance

orders in other parts of the United Kingdom), at the end there shall be added the "words or an order for financial provision in the form of a monetary payment under section 8 of the Family Law (Scotland) Act 1985".

The Succession (Scotland) Act 1964 (c. 41)

4. In section 33(2) of the Succession (Scotland) Act 1964 (construction of references to legal rights in marriage contracts), at the end there shall be added the words "or section 8 of the Family Law (Scotland) Act 1985".

The Law Reform (Miscellaneous Provisions) (Scotland) Act 1966 (c. 19)

5. In section 8(1) of the Law Reform (Miscellaneous Provisions) (Scotland) Act 1966 (variation and recall of certain orders regarding custody and maintenance), at the end of paragraph (c) there shall be added the words "or section 8 of the Family Law (Scotland) Act 1985".

The Maintenance Orders (Reciprocal Enforcement) Act 1972 (c. 18)

6. In section 31 of the Maintenance Orders (Reciprocal Enforcement) Act 1972 (application by person in convention country for recovery of maintenance in Scotland
    (a) for subsection (1A) there shall be substituted the following subsections—
        "(1A) Proceedings arising out of an application under subsection (1) above shall be treated as an action for aliment within the meaning of the Family Law (Scotland) Act 1985 and, subject to subsections (1B) to (1D) below, the provisions of that Act relating to aliment shall apply in relation to claims for maintenance in such proceedings and decrees therein.
        (1B) Without prejudice to subsection (2) below, any proceedings mentioned in subsection (IA) above shall be brought in the sheriff court.
        (1C) In its application to proceedings mentioned in subsection (1 A) above, section 5 of the said Act of 1985 (power to vary or recall decree of aliment) shall be subject to section 34(1) of this Act.
        (1D) Where an application under subsection (1) above is for the recovery of maintenance from a person who is a former spouse of the applicant—
        (a) then, for the purposes of the said Act of 1985, there shall be assumed to be an obligation of aliment within the meaning of that Act owed by the former spouse to the applicant;
        (b) section 2(7) and (8); of that Act shall not apply: and
        (c) an order for payment of maintenance in proceedings arising out of the application—
            (i) shall, if subsisting at the death of the party making the payment, continue to operate against that party's estate, but without prejudice to the power of the court to vary or recall the order; and
            (ii) shall cease to have effect on the remarriage or death of the party receiving payment except in relation to any arrears due under it;
    (b) after subsection (4) there shall be inserted the following new subsection—
        "(4A) In subsection (4)(i) above the reference to the dissolution of a marriage by divorce shall be construed as including a reference to the annulment of a purported marriage and any reference to a marriage, a divorce, a divorced person, a former spouse or divorce proceedings shall be construed accordingly."; and
    (c) subsection (5) shall cease to have effect.
7. In section 39 of that Act, in the definition of "maintenance", for the words "as a periodical allowance" there shall be substituted the words "by one former spouse for the support of the other".

The Matrimonial Proceedings (Polygamous Marriages) Act 1972 (c. 38)

8. In section 2(2) of the Matrimonial Proceedings (Polygamous Marriages) Act 1972 (decrees in respect of polygamous marriages)—
    (a) for paragraphs (d) and (e) there shall be substituted the following paragraphs—
        "(d) a decree of separation;
        (e) a decree of aliment;"; and
    (b) after the word "ancillary" there shall be inserted the words "or incidental".

The Domicile and Matrimonial Proceedings Act 1973 *(c. 45)*

9. In Schedule 2 to the Domicile and Matrimonial Proceedings Act 1973 (ancillary and collateral orders)—

    (a) before paragraph 3, there shall be inserted the following paragraphs
        "2A. Any enactment or rule of law empowering a court to make an order for payment of aliment (including interim aliment)."; and

    (b) after paragraph 12A, there shall be inserted the following paragraph—
        "12B. Section 8 (orders for financial provision on divorce), section 17(1) (financial provision on declarator of nullity of marriage) and section 18 (orders relating to avoidance transactions) of the Family Law (Scotland) Act 1985."

The Land Registration *(Scotland)* Act 1979 *(c. 33)*

10. In section 12(3)(b) of the Land Registration (Scotland) Act 1979 (circumstances in which there is no entitlement to indemnity for loss), at the end there shall be added the words "or has been set aside or varied by an order under section 18(2) (orders relating to avoidance transactions) of the Family Law (Scotland) Act 1985".

The Matrimonial Homes *(Family Protection) (Scotland)* Act 1981 *(c. 59)*

11. For section 13(2) of the Matrimonial Homes (Family Protection) (Scotland) Act 1981 (transfer of tenancy) there shall be substituted the following subsection—

    "(2) In an action—
    (a) for divorce, the Court of Session or a sheriff;
    (b) for nullity of marriage, the Court of Session,
may, on granting decree or within such period as the court may specify on granting decree, make an order granting an application under subsection (1) above."

The Matrimonial and Family Proceedings Act 1984 *(c. 42)*

12. After section 29 of the Matrimonial and Family Proceedings Act 1984 there shall be inserted the following new section—

"Application of Part IV to annulled marriages
    29A. This Part of this Act shall apply to an annulment, of whatever nature, of a purported marriage, as it applies to a divorce, and references to marriage and divorce shall be construed accordingly.".

13. In section 30(1) of that Act (interpretation of Part IV), in the definition of "order for financial provision", for the words from "paragraphs (a)" to "1976" there shall be substituted the words "section 8(1) of the Family Law (Scotland) Act 1985".

REPEALS

Chapter	Short title	Extent of repeal
24 & 25 Vict. c.86.	The Conjugal Rights (Scotland) Amendment Act 1861.	In section 6, the words from "be held and considered" to "as if she were unmarried. and": the words "the same shall": and the words from "provided that if any such wife" to the end of the section. In section 9, the word "maintenance". Sections 15 and 16.
44 & 45 Vict. c.21.	The Married Women's Property (Scotland) Act 1881.	Sections 1 to 5. Section 8. The Schedule.
10 & 11 Geo. 5. c.54.	The Married Women's Property (Scotland) Act 1920.	The whole Act.
15 & 16 Geo. 5 c.45.	The Guardianship of Infants Act 1925.	Section 3(2). In section 5(4), the words from "and may further order" to the end of the subsection. Section 8.
20 & 21 Geo. 5. c.33.	The Illegitimate Children (Scotland) Act 1930	Section 1. In section 2, in subsection (1). the words "or in any action for aliment for an illegitimate child", and subsection (2). Section 3. Section 5.
22 & 23 Geo. 5. c.47.	The Children and Young Persons (Scotland) Act 1932.	Section 73(1)(*b*) and (3).
2 & 3 Geo. 6. c.4.	The Custody of Children (Scotland) Act 1939.	In section 1, in subsection (1) the word "maintenance" and subsection (2).
14 Geo. 6. c.37.	The Maintenance Orders Act 1950.	Section 6(2). In section 7, the words from "whether" to "maintenance of the pupil child".
15 & 16 Geo. 6 & 1 Eliz. 2. c.41	The Affiliation Orders Act 1952.	The whole Act.
6 & 7 Eliz. 2. c.40.	The Matrimonial Proceedings (Children) Act 1958.	In section 7, in subsection (1), the word "maintenance", and subsection (2). In section 9(1), the word "maintenance".
1964 c.19.	The Married Women's Property Act 1964.	The whole Act.
1972 c.18.	The Maintenance Orders (Reciprocal Enforcement) Act 1972.	Section 31(5).
1973 c.45.	The Domicile and Matrimonial Proceedings Act 1973.	In Schedule 2, paragraphs 1 and 2.
1976 c.39.	The Divorce (Scotland) Act 1976.	Sections 5 to 8.
1978 c.22.	The Domestic Proceedings and Magistrates' Courts Act 1978.	Section 60(1)(a). In Schedule 2, paragraph 1(a).
1981 c.59.	The Matrimonial Homes (Family Protection) (Scotland) Act 1981.	Section 7(5).
1982 c.27.	The Civil Jurisdiction and Judgments Act 1982.	In paragraph 1 of Schedule 9, the words "for adherence and aliment or"
1983 c.12.	The Divorce Jurisdiction, Court Fees ad Legal Aid (Scotland) Act 1983.	In Schedule 1, paragraphs 21 and 23.

Family Law Scotland Act 1985

Chapter	Short title	Extent of repeal
1984 c.15.	The Law Reform (Husband and Wife) (Scotland) Act 1984.	In Schedule 1, paragraphs 3, 4 and 6.

Appendix

McConnell v. McConnell (No. 2) 60
Jackson v. Jackson 70
R v. R 83

McCONNELL v. McCONNELL (No. 2)

Second Division, November 30, 1994. Reported 1997 Fam.L.R. 108.

OPINION OF THE LORD JUSTICE CLERK (ROSS)

...Counsel for the defender made it plain that no challenge was being made to the interlocutor of August 19, 1993 insofar as it granted decree of divorce, dealt with the custody of and aliment for the children, transferred to the pursuer the defender's right in 4 Barnton Avenue West, transferred various items to the defender, and ordered the defender to arrange the discharge of the whole debt secured over 4 Barnton Avenue West. Counsel did however intimate that they would move the court to recall the Lord Ordinary's interlocutor quoad payment of a capital sum of £50,000 and in relation to the award of periodical allowance. Grounds of appeal have been lodged on behalf of the defender. Ground 1 is in general terms, and counsel intimated that they were no longer seeking to support ground 2. The remaining grounds are in the following terms:

> "3. The Lord Ordinary failed to treat the nature, use, etc of (a) the defender's loan to CDG (Scotland) and (b) the defender's shareholding in CDG (Scotland) as a 'special circumstance' in terms of s 10(1) and [(6)(d)] of the Act justifying departure from the principle of equal sharing. In so doing he erred. In any event the Lord Ordinary erred in valuing said assets without allowing for the incidence of tax.
> 4. The Lord Ordinary erred in failing to address the reasonableness test laid down in s 8(2) of the Act. He had no regard to the evident disparity at the date of proof between the realisable values of property in the hands of or to be transferred to the pursuer and defender respectively. The capital sum ordered to be paid was by itself or taken with other financial provision wholly unreasonable and contrary to s 8(2) of the Act.
> 5. The Lord Ordinary erred in making an order for periodical allowance without applying the statutory test laid down in s 13(2) of the Act. The order for periodical allowance was by itself or taken with other financial provision wholly unreasonable and contrary to s 8(2) of the Act.
> 6. The financial provision should be reviewed with the effect of recalling the order for capital payment and/or the order for periodical allowance failing which by reducing the quantum of capital payment and/or periodical allowance".

The Lord Ordinary has written a very lengthy opinion in this case dealing with *inter alia* the relevant facts, and there is no need to repeat these now. Suffice it to say that a considerable time at the proof was taken up with questions relating to the valuation of various items of matrimonial property. The Lord Ordinary in his long and careful opinion has described the decision at which he has arrived in relation to these issues of valuation, and the parties have now accepted the Lord Ordinary's valuations. In his opinion the Lord Ordinary lists the items of matrimonial property which were either agreed or determined by him as well as all liabilities which required to be taken into account. The matrimonial property had a total value of £1,450,044. The Lord Ordinary then proceeded to list the items of matrimonial property which were held by the pursuer at the relevant date.

These were stated as follows:

(1) a one half share of Almond Lodge, 4 Barnton Avenue West, Edinburgh	£262,500.00
(2) a one half share of the contents of the Woolwich Building Society account	£52,787.00
(3) a one half share of the Royal Bank of Scotland current account	£435.00
(4) pursuer's shares in quoted companies	£1,900.00
(5) a one half share of the contents of Almond Lodge, 4 Barnton Avenue West, Edinburgh	£10,000.00
(6) pursuer's car	£4,000.00
Total	**£331,622.00**

The Lord Ordinary then listed the matrimonial property in the hands of the defender as follows:

(1) a one half share of Almond Lodge, 4 Barnton Avenue West, Edinburgh	£262,500.00

(2) Bank of Scotland deposit account in the name of the defender	£276,636.00
(3) a one half share of the contents of the Woolwich Building Society account	£52,786.00
(4) Halifax Building Society account	£78,410.00
(5) a one half share of the Royal Bank of Scotland current account	£434.00
(6) life and pension policies of the defender	£18,300.00
(7) defender's shares in quoted companies	£1,900.00
(8) a one half share of the contents of Almond Lodge, 4 Barnton Avenue West, Edinburgh	£10,000.00
(9) director's loan by the defender to Comprehensive Development Group (Scotland) and accrued interest thereon	£267,456
(10) defender's 60 per cent shareholding in Comprehensive Total Development Group (Scotland)	£150,000
Total	**£1,118,422.00**

The Lord Ordinary next listed the relevant debts of the parties of which he required to take account in terms of s 10(2) of the Act of 1985. These were listed as follows:

(1) mortgage over Almond Lodge, 4 Barnton Avenue West, Edinburgh	£37,456.00
(2) defender's income tax liabilities	£89,381.00
(3) defender's obligation to children in respect of their inheritance	£14,500.00
Total	**£141,337.00**

The Lord Ordinary observed that of these debts one half of the debt due under the mortgage, namely £18,728, is the responsibility of the pursuer. The remaining debts amounting in total to £122,609 were the responsibility of the defender.

Having regard to the foregoing figures, the Lord Ordinary pointed out that the net value of the matrimonial property amounted to £1,308.707. Of this, £312,894 was in the hands of the pursuer and £995,813 was in the hands of the defender.

In his opinion the Lord Ordinary observed that the defender was content that whatever liability the court might determine him to have towards the Pursuer, it could be satisfied at least in part by a transfer to her of his one half pro indiviso share of Almond Lodge, 4 Barnton Avenue West, Edinburgh, and his presumed half share in the contents of Almond Lodge. The Lord Ordinary also observed that on the basis of the figures quoted above, to achieve equal sharing, there required to be transferred from the defender to the pursuer property to the value of £341,460. If there were transferred to the pursuer the defender's share of Almond Lodge, and his share of the contents therein, that would involve a transfer of value of £272,500. That would leave an amount of £68,959 which the Lord Ordinary rounded up to £70,000 due by the defender to the pursuer if equal sharing was to be achieved.

The Lord Ordinary went on to point out that the pursuer would no doubt welcome the discharge of the mortgage debt secured over Almond Lodge at the time. That debt amounts to £37,456, and each party is liable for one half of the debt. Accordingly if the defender were to discharge the pursuer's share of the debt, along with his share of the debt, the result would be that there would still remain a necessity for transfer of value of £50,000 in round figures by the defender to the pursuer if equal sharing was to be achieved. The Lord Ordinary concluded that equal sharing should be achieved, and for that reason he made an order for payment of a capital sum by the defender to the pursuer of an amount of £50,000. That decision of the Lord Ordinary is now challenged, and counsel for the defender maintained that in the circumstances the Lord Ordinary should not have ordered the defender to make payment of that sum. The question of whether or not the Lord Ordinary should have ordered the defender to make payment of this sum depends upon the question of whether he was well founded in holding that there should be equal sharing, or whether there were special circumstances justifying a departure from an equal sharing of the net value of the matrimonial property.

In order to determine this issue, it is necessary to have regard to the provisions of the Family Law (Scotland) Act 1985. [His Lordship narrated the terms of sections 8, 9 and 10 and continued:]

In his opinion the Lord Ordinary observes that various submissions were made to him on behalf of the pursuer and the defender as to the manner in which the matrimonial property ought to be shared between the parties. He added: "However, as I understood them, none of those submissions involved, the suggestion that I should depart significantly from the equal sharing desiderated by s 10(1) of the Act of 1985, in the absence of 'special circumstances' ".

The Lord Ordinary went on to say that having carefully considered all the evidence relevant to that matter, he reached the conclusion that there were no special circumstances in the case such as would justify a departure from an equal sharing of the net value of the matrimonial property. In those circumstances the Lord Ordinary pronounced the interlocutor of August 19, 1993 which provided *inter alia* for the payment to the pursuer of the sum of £50,000. Counsel for the defender's first submission was that the Lord Ordinary had been in error in concluding that there were no special circumstances such as to justify a departure from an equal sharing of the net value of the matrimonial property, and that accordingly he should not have granted decree in favour of the pursuer for payment of £50,000. In her very careful submissions, junior counsel for the defender advanced a number of reasons in support of the contention that the Lord Ordinary had erred in concluding that there were no special reasons in the case to justify a departure from equal sharing. Counsel accepted that the terms of the statute made it plain that division into equal shares was presumed to be fair, but contended that that presumption would be displaced by proof of special circumstances which rendered a division into equal shards as unfair. In this connection, the submissions turned upon the terms of s 10(6)(d), and the court was invited to consider the nature of the matrimonial property, the use of it and the extent to which it was reasonable to expect it to be realised. Submissions to the effect that it was not reasonable to expect items of the matrimonial property to be realised were advanced in relation to the defender's loans to the company and his shareholding. The proposition was that both these items would on any view be difficult to realise, and that since that was so, this demonstrated that special circumstances existed justifying a departure from equal sharing. We were informed that if the order for payment of a capital sum of £50,000 was not made, this would result in the matrimonial property being shared in the proportions of approximately 46 per cent to the pursuer and 54 per cent to the defender.

Counsel for the defender further submitted that the Lord Ordinary had erred in failing to address the test of reasonableness contained in s 8(2) of the Act of 1985. Alternatively, if he did address that test, he erred in concluding that the award made was reasonable; such a conclusion was wholly unreasonable having regard to the parties' relative resources.

Counsel also contended that the Lord Ordinary had erred in making any award of periodical allowance at all. He would only be entitled to make such an award if he was satisfied that an order would be justified by the principles laid down in s 9(1)(d) of the Act of 1985, and further if he were satisfied that the order for a capital sum or the transfer of property would be inappropriate or insufficient to satisfy the requirements of s 8(2). Counsel maintained that it was plain from the Lord Ordinary's opinion that he had disregarded the provisions of s 13(2)(b) of the Act of 1985 as he had made no reference whatsoever to the fact that property was being transferred to the pursuer. Part of the property transferred consisted of the development site at 4 Barnton Avenue, and the Lord Ordinary gave no explanation whatsoever for disregarding the income which could be obtained from that portion of the property transferred to the pursuer. Counsel maintained that it was necessary to consider what other resources she had before making any order for periodical allowance. When regard was had to all the resources available to the pursuer, it was contended that it would not be reasonable to make any award of periodical allowance to her. This would be so particularly if the award to her of £50,000 in addition to the transfer of property was made.

Counsel for the pursuer on the other hand maintained that the Lord Ordinary's decision was one which he was entitled to make. They emphasised that the Lord Ordinary was exercising a discretion. and that this court should be slow to interfere with such exercise of discretion. Counsel further submitted that the Lord Ordinary, had made no finding one way or the other on the subject of realisability, and that accordingly there was no justification for holding that there were special circumstances in terms of s 10(6)(d) of the Act of 1985. Counsel then considered the evidence in relation to both the shareholding in the company and the loans to the company and maintained that on the evidence the Lord Ordinary was not bound to find that there would be any difficulty in realising either the loan or the shareholding in the company. So far as the shareholding was concerned the relative lack of a market for such shares had been taken into account when arriving at the value of the shares, and accordingly the proper conclusion was that the shares could be realised at such a discounted value.

So far as the resources of the parties were concerned, counsel for the pursuer maintained that it was plain from the evidence that the defender had sufficient resources to make payment of the award made, and that accordingly the award made was a reasonable one.

As regards periodical allowance, counsel maintained that it was clear from the terms of the Act that the court could make an order for periodical allowance even where the court had ordered payment to be made of a substantial capital sum. They contended that the Lord Ordinary was entitled to make an order for payment of a periodical allowance, and that in doing so he was exercising a discretion. He had ordered the periodic allowance to be paid for a period of three years, and he was entitled to make such an order. Counsel further submitted that if that period of three years was to be reduced on the ground that the pursuer had been given other resources from which she could derive an income including the £50,000 and the development site at 4 Barnton Avenue, the minimum period for periodical allowance should not be reduced below 18 months, in order to give her ample time to market the development land in the most favourable way.

It was not disputed that there is a presumption in favour of equal sharing of the net value of the matrimonial property. Unless there are special circumstances, it is to be divided equally between a husband and wife. A number of special circumstances are listed in s 10(6) of the Act of 1985, although the list is not exhaustive.

In the present case, the defender has founded upon s 10(6)(d). The special circumstances are said to have been the defender's shareholding in the company and his loans to the company, and the submission is that these would not be easy to realise with the result that it would not be reasonable to expect them to be realised.

In giving his evidence in relation to the valuation of the defender's shareholding in the company, Mr Gilbert stated that having regard to the circumstances existing at the time, it would have been very hard to find a purchaser for the company at all, and it was partly for this reason that he opted for an assets basis valuation. The Lord Ordinary accepted Mr Gilbert's valuation and I am satisfied that the evidence did demonstrate that the defender's shareholding in the company could not reasonably be expected to be realised at the relevant date. Mr Gilbert valued on an assets basis because there was no market for the shares; the company was a private unlimited company in which the defender was the major shareholder; the shares could not be sold piecemeal; if any sale was to take place, it would have had to be the sale of his whole shareholding. Moreover, if shares were sold, claims for capital gains tax would arise. It was suggested on behalf of the pursuer that capital gains tax could be mitigated by taking the consideration for the shares sold in the form of shares in the acquiring company, but that would not be practicable when the shares were being sold to realise funds with which to meet the pursuer's claim for a capital sum.

On the evidence, I am in no doubt that it would not have been reasonable to expect the defender's shareholding to be realised. Insofar as the loans to the company are concerned, the evidence made it plain that the loans to the company by the defender and his partner, Mr Low, were to provide working capital for the company. It was suggested on the pursuer's behalf that the loans could be reduced by the company taking loans from a bank or other lending institution. There was, however, evidence from the defender and Mr Low to the effect that the company had a policy of not borrowing from a bank. In my opinion, the proper effect of the evidence is that there might be difficulty in realising the full loan, and that accordingly the defender's loans to the company were not an item of matrimonial property which it was reasonable to expect to be realised *in toto*. There was, however, evidence to which I shall refer presently to the effect that there was some prospect of the loans being realised in part.

In his opinion, the Lord Ordinary stated: "Having carefully considered all of the evidence relevant to the matter, I have reached the conclusion that there are no special circumstances in this case such as would justify a departure from an equal sharing of the net value of the matrimonial property."

Although the Lord Ordinary states that he has considered all the evidence, he makes no express reference to either the shareholding or the loans to the company in this connection, and in my opinion, when the evidence regarding these two items is considered, the proper conclusion is that it would not be reasonable to expect them to be realised.

The question then arises as to whether, in the light of that evidence, the Lord Ordinary was entitled to conclude that there were no special circumstances justifying a departure from equal sharing or whether he ought to have held that unequal sharing was justified by special circumstances.

In the course of their submissions, it was submitted by counsel for the defenders that since part of the matrimonial property was of such a nature that it was not reasonable to expect it to be realised, that necessarily meant that there were special circumstances justifying a departure from equal sharing. Counsel for the pursuers, on the other hand, emphasised that the Lord Ordinary had a discretion in determining whether there were special circumstances, and they maintained that if there was no reasonable expectation that the shareholding and the loans would have to be reduced in order to satisfy the claim for a capital sum, then no question of special circumstances could arise.

In my opinion, when it is established in relation to some items of matrimonial property that it would not be reasonable to expect them to be realised in order to satisfy any claim for payment of a capital sum, it is a question of circumstances and degree whether that constitutes special circumstances justifying a departure from equal sharing. A number of different situations can be envisaged. The husband may have various items of matrimonial property many of which are capable of easy realisation, and a small part only of which may be such that it is not reasonable to expect it to be realised. in such a situation, special circumstances in terms of s 10(6)(d) will not arise. In *Little v. Little,* 1990 S.L.T. 785, the matrimonial property included pension rights which both parties had. At 788 the Lord President said: "The values attached to each party's interest represented the actuarial value of their prospective entitlement under the scheme at the relevant date, not cash in hand. The nature of the scheme is such that neither interest will be capable of being realised for cash of equivalent value at any stage, since a substantial part of the benefit is represented by the pension. Clearly, matrimonial property of this character requires careful attention if it is to be shared fairly between the parties in a settlement on divorce, and it would be a serious error if the court were to assume that an equal and instant division of the actuarial value was capable of being made as if it were cash in hand. On the other hand there may be cases where there are other realisable assets of sufficient value which can be drawn upon to achieve that result, and if so it may well be appropriate to take the full actuarial value into account in achieving the division in the knowledge that the party who makes the payment has other resources on which he or she can draw."

In my opinion the principle laid down in that passage is of general application. On the other hand, where the husband has assets a large proportion of which are of such a nature that it would not be reasonable to expect them to be realised, it may be that special circumstances in terms of s 10(6)(d) will be held to exist so as to justify unequal sharing.

In the present case, at the relevant date, in addition to his one half share in the property at 4 Barnton Avenue West, and his shareholding in the company and his loans to the company, the defender had £276,636 on deposit account with the Bank of Scotland, a one half share of the contents of the Woolwich Building Society account amounting to £52,786 and £78,410 in an account with the Halifax Building Society. Accordingly, even accepting that the shareholding and the loans to the company could not readily be realised, if the defender was required to pay a capital sum of £50,000 to the pursuer in addition to the transfer of property he had other assets on which he could draw to meet that payment and also the payment necessary to discharge the mortgage over 4 Barnton Avenue West.

It was submitted on behalf of the defender that the evidence showed that these sums in bank and building society accounts were earmarked for specific purposes. The £276,636 was said to be earmarked by him for the purchase of a house, the amount in the Halifax building society was earmarked to meet tax liabilities and the amount in the Woolwich building society account was intended to meet his overdraft and legal fees. The evidence established that after the separation, the defender in fact bought for himself a house in Ann Street for £273,000. For the pursuer it was suggested that it was unnecessary for him to have spent so much money in obtaining a house for himself. However that may be, it is plain that at the relevant date the defender had resources other than the loan and shareholding from which he could have made payment of the capital sum of £50.000 to the pursuer and could have discharged the mortgage over 4 Barnton Avenue West. That being so, I am not persuaded that the Lord Ordinary was bound to hold that there were special circumstances justifying a departure from equal sharing.

But matters do not end there. It was not disputed that in terms of s 8(2)(b) the order which the court makes must be reasonable having regard to the resources of the parties. Although there was evidence that it was company policy not to take loans from banks or lending institutions, the defender accepted that he could have imposed upon the company a change of policy requiring the company to look to other lenders to take on part at least of the loans made by him. In particular he accepted that if such a change of policy was imposed by him, the company could hope to borrow against the security of the company's property in Glasgow which is worth approximately £250,000. The defender himself stated that the bank would lend about 60 per cent of the value of that property, that is, £150,000 on the security of that property. Having regard to the extent of the defender's interest in the company, if that were done he could then expect to receive repayment of his loan to the extent of £90,000 with the balance of £60,000 being used to repay loans made by Mr Low. Counsel for the defender informed us that it had been agreed before the Lord Ordinary that such a figure of £90,000 might reasonably be expected to be realised by the defender by loan substitution in this way. In these circumstances, it appears to me that the court is entitled to proceed upon the view that it is reasonable to expect £90,000 of the defender's loans to the company to be realised by loan substitution. Accordingly, the defender could employ that sum of £90,000 to make payment to the pursuer of the capital sum of £50,000 and at the same time to discharge both his and the pursuer's liability for the mortgage over 4 Barnton Avenue West. All this could be achieved without requiring the shareholding to be sold and without necessitating any calling up of the balance of the defender's loans to the company. This serves to confirm me in my conclusion that the Lord Ordinary was well entitled to hold that special circumstances justifying a departure from equal sharing had not been established.

I fully recognise that the Lord Ordinary has not given detailed reasons for his conclusion regarding special circumstances. However, I accept, as counsel accepted, that he was not addressed upon this matter to the same extent as this court was. However that may be I am satisfied that having regard to the evidence, he was entitled to reach the conclusion which he did. Indeed, even if it were held that because the Lord Ordinary had failed to give reasons, the matter was at large for this court, I am satisfied that special circumstances have not been made out justifying a departure from equal sharing.

I am also satisfied in terms of s 8(2)(b) of the Act of 1985, that having regard to the resources of both parties, the award of £50,000 should be regarded as reasonable in the circumstances. In my opinion the defender's challenge of the award of £50,000 must fail. The defender also challenged the award of periodical allowance on the ground that the Lord Ordinary had failed to apply the test laid down in s 13(2)(b) of the Act of 1985.

I have already set forth the provisions of s 9(1)(d), and the Lord Ordinary makes it plain in his opinion that it was on reliance upon the provisions of that subsection that he made the award of periodical allowance in the pursuer's favour for a period of three years. Counsel for the defender maintained that the Lord Ordinary had failed properly to apply the test laid down in s 13(2) (b). Counsel submitted that when regard was had to the payment o the capital sum and transfer of property made in favour of the pursuer, it could not reasonably be concluded that these would be insufficient to satisfy the requirements of s 8(2). Counsel submitted that there was no justification for any payment of periodical allowance at all, or alternatively that it should be for a shorter period than three years.

The effect of the legislation is that a court may not award periodical allowance unless it is satisfied that an order for the payment of a capital sum or transfer of property would be inappropriate or insufficient, and that the order for periodical allowance is justified by at least one of the principles laid down in s 9(1)(c)-(e). As already observed, in the present case what is relied on is s 9(1)(d). For the defender it was submitted that the Lord Ordinary's approach to periodical allowance was defective in two respects. First, although in making the award he purported to have regard to the amount of capital sum which he proposed to award, he had not attached sufficient weight to the fact that the pursuer was going to receive £50,000 in cash in addition to the transfer of property in her favour. Secondly, in making the award of periodical allowance the Lord Ordinary failed to attach proper weight to the fact that the pursuer was having transferred to her the property at 4 Barnton Avenue West which included the development site.

Again the Lord Ordinary's opinion upon this matter is fairly brief, no doubt because the submissions made to him were less elaborate than those addressed to this court. The Lord Ordinary plainly did have regard to the fact that the pursuer was to have transferred to her the subject at 4 Barnton Avenue West because he recognised that in due course she might well consider it appropriate for her to realise some of the very considerable amount of capital which it represented. He concluded that she should be given a reasonable time within which to adjust to the new circumstances.

In my opinion, it is clear that the Lord Ordinary has not given proper weight to the fact that in addition to having transferred to her the defender's share in 4 Barnton Avenue West which is the matrimonial home, the pursuer is to receive a sum of £50,000. I think there is force in the defender's argument that that sum is available to support the pursuer during the period when she requires to adjust to the new situation which will obtain once the divorce is granted. It could obviously be invested so as to produce some income for her support, and I shall return to this matter in due course. More importantly, however, I am satisfied that the Lord Ordinary has failed to attach proper weight to the evidence in relation to the development site at 4 Barnton Avenue West.

[His Lordship summarised the evidence and continued:]

I am satisfied that it is reasonable to conclude that once there has been the transfer of property to the pursuer, she will be able to retain the matrimonial home as a home for herself and her children, and immediately realise the development site for a sum of approximately £175,000. When that sum is added to the sum of £50,000 which she is also to receive from the defender she will have a capital sum totalling £225,000 which can be invested to provide her with an income.

In my opinion the Lord Ordinary erred in not appreciating that the pursuer would be in a position to realise the development site fairly quickly, and that thereafter the proceeds of that realisation plus the £50,000 of capital awarded to her would be available for her support. The Lord Ordinary stated that the periodical allowance which he proposed to award would give the pursuer an opportunity to consider her future arrangements, but I am not persuaded that she requires a period of three years to do so. I accept that there was no direct evidence to the effect that it would be possible to sell the development site immediately, but in my opinion, the general tenor of the evidence must be that the development site was an asset of considerable value which could be realised in the very near future. At the present time it produces no income at all. In these circumstances I have considered carefully whether there is any justification for an award of periodical allowance at all in this case. A strong case can be made out for making no award, but I have come to the conclusion that it would be reasonable, to enable the pursuer to adjust to the new situation and to sell the development site, to award periodical allowance for a period of six months.

A question must then arise as to the amount of any award of periodical allowance. The Lord Ordinary awarded periodical allowance at the rate of £1,200 per month, although again he gives no reasons for selecting that figure. As I understand it, however, the figure awarded is less than the amount awarded for interim aliment, and it may be that the Lord Ordinary has selected a smaller figure having regard to the fact that the pursuer is to receive on divorce payment of a capital sum of £50,000. However that may be, the question of the amount to be awarded for periodical allowance was very much a matter for the Lord Ordinary's discretion, and I do not feel justified in disturbing the figure which he awarded although I am not persuaded that he was entitled to award that amount for as long a period as three years. In the circumstances, I would move your Lordships to grant the reclaiming motion to the extent of substituting a period of six months for a period of three years as the period during which periodical allowance will be paid; quoad ultra I would move your Lordships to affirm the interlocutor of the Lord Ordinary.

OPINION OF LORD McCLUSKEY

... The Lord Ordinary, it was said, had clearly given no adequate consideration to the vital questions of realisability and reasonableness before pronouncing himself satisfied that there were no special circumstances such as would justify a departure from equal sharing of the net value of the matrimonial property. It was not even clear whether that view of the Lord Ordinary was based on the conclusion that there were no special circumstances, or, alternatively, that there were special circumstances but they were not such special circumstances as to justify a departure from the principle of equal sharing. In reply, counsel for the respondent pointed out that s 10(6)(d) was concerned exclusively with matrimonial property—as defined in s 10(4). Item 2 on the list of matrimonial property held by the reclaimer was a cash sum of £276,636. That sum did not require to be "realised"; it was a liquid asset at the only material date, namely the relevant date, and was available to enable the reclaimer to pay £50,000 without difficulty. He had no need to realise either of [the company loan or shares]. In addition, it was submitted that the evidence and the concession by counsel for the reclaimer showed that £90,000 of the loan could be realised without undue difficulty. Accordingly, applying the observations of the Lord President in *Little v. Little,* 1990 S.L.T. 785 at 788L to 789A, this was plainly a case in which there were "other realisable assets of sufficient value" which could be drawn upon to achieve the intended result, namely equal sharing of the net value of the matrimonial property. Thus it was evident that without having to realise any item of the matrimonial property that might be difficult to realise the reclaimer could pay the £50,000. The fact that he had, subsequent to the relevant date, chosen to use the £276,636 to purchase a house was of no relevance, in that s 10(6)(d) was concerned only with matrimonial property. The house at Ann Street had never been matrimonial property; so its realisation did not arise.

In my opinion, the submission for the respondent on this point is so clearly correct that the reclaimer's motion must fail, even if he is entirely correct in his assertion that the general character of the other items of matrimonial property held by him is different from the general character of the matrimonial property items held by the respondent and that it would not be reasonable to expect [the loan or the shares] to be realised whether in whole or in part. It is quite true that the result of the various orders made by the Lord Ordinary is that the respondent's assets were, for the most part, more readily realisable than those of the reclaimer, in the sense that they could be more readily converted into cash. But the biggest cash asset of all forming part of the matrimonial property was the £276,636 bank deposit which was held by the reclaimer at the relevant date. Thus if he had to pay £50,000 to the respondent he could do so without difficulty; and no question of realising the loan or the shares would arise. There are plainly no special circumstances within the meaning of s 10(6)(d) which relate to the bank deposit, a cash item. In the light of the Lord President's opinion in *Little* it follows in my opinion that there are no special circumstances here justifying any departure from the principle of equal sharing. The Lord Ordinary's conclusion was accordingly correct and the reclaiming motion in relation to the sharing of the net value of the matrimonial property must be refused.

On the question of the periodical allowance, it is now clear that the Lord Ordinary's treatment of the matter requires to be reconsidered in the light of the whole circumstances emerging from the resolution of the valuation and sharing questions. Section 13(2) prohibits the making of an order for periodical allowance unless the court "is satisfied that an order for payment of a capital sum or for transfer of property under that (s 8(2)) would be inappropriate or insufficient to satisfy the requirements of the said s 8(2)".

[His Lordship narrated the terms of s 8(2) and continued:]

Thus the relevant principles of s 9 are brought into the matter. These provisions plainly require the court to consider whether or not the making of the other orders render the award or the periodical allowance unnecessary or inappropriate. In this case, the Lord Ordinary made an order (which is not challenged) to transfer to the respondent the reclaimer's right, title and interest in Almond Lodge, 4 Barnton Avenue West, Edinburgh. That item of heritable property included certain garden ground which the Lord Ordinary found to be separable from the rest of the subjects and saleable for a sum of not less than £175,000, and possibly for as much as £225,000, if full planning permissions were to be obtained. There was nothing in the evidence to establish that this separable asset would be difficult to sell. Furthermore, its most significant feature is that, unsold and remaining part of the Almond Lodge subjects occupied by the respondent, it would not be income-producing: it would be lying fallow. The evidence does not suggest that its capital value would be increasing or decreasing while it lay fallow. If it were sold, however, and the proceeds were to be invested even at the modest interest rates now available it could yield a very substantial sum of money each year. This being so, the Lord Ordinary should have considered carefully whether or not it was reasonable within the meaning of s 9(1)(d) to require the reclaimer to pay the respondent a periodical allowance while the respondent neglected to put this valuable asset to use as an income-generator. The Lord Ordinary did not expressly consider this. It appears that he may not have considered it at all: it is easy to understand why not because the relevant considerations were hardly, if at all, canvassed before him. Nonetheless, they were canvassed before us and we must determine this point.

In my opinion, it would be unconscionable to allow the respondent to have this asset of matrimonial property and, at the reclaimer's expense, to neglect to realise its income-generating potential. It may be, as suggested by her counsel, that she would be slow to sell off this plot when there was a risk that there might be built upon the site a development which she might find obtrusive in relation to her occupation of the main house and ground. That may be so, though it is entirely speculative. In this matter the onus rests upon the respondent. I can see no reason why she should be allowed to neglect this asset and at the same time receive an alimentary payment from the reclaimer. If that were done he would in effect be paying to allow her to refrain from testing the market for this plot of land. Furthermore, as a result of the award of the £50,000 balancing cash payment, which we are confirming, and her other assets, the respondent is relatively cash rich. Even without encroaching upon her capital she can generate a substantial income from her liquid assets.

In these circumstances I can see no warrant for an award of a periodical allowance for a period of three years. No doubt, as the Lord Ordinary recognised, it would be sensible to give the respondent a reasonable time to realise the value of the asset consisting of the separable site. We had various submissions about what period might be appropriate; but these submissions were not well supported by the evidence, which appears to be very slight on this matter. As I have indicated, this is a matter in respect of which the onus rests upon the respondent. Although the evidence tells us very little; it gives no support for the view that it would be difficult, or would take a long time, to realise the value of this site. In these circumstances, I can see no justification for any award of periodical allowance beyond a six month period commencing with the date of the interlocutor in this reclaiming motion. As to the amount. the Lord Ordinary chose £1,200 per month. In arriving at that figure it is not clear that he made any allowance for the income which could be immediately obtained from a safe investment of the £50,000 which the reclaimer was ordered to pay the respondent; even at 7 per cent, that sum would produce approximately £300 per month. In my view, therefore, a periodical allowance of £900 per month for the six months period might have been more appropriate. However, as your Lordships consider that the figure of £1,200 was one that the Lord Ordinary was entitled to choose, I will not dissent from that view.

The reclaimer also submitted that we could also have regard to the respondent's earning capacity. This is not a very significant item. But in any event it is one which the Lord Ordinary considered and it has not been shown that he erred in concluding that, in this respect the respondent should be given a period of time to adjust to her new circumstances created by the determination of these proceedings.

OPINION OF LORD MORISON

... In my opinion it is clearly established by the evidence that withdrawal of the loan, which constitutes a substantial part of the working capital of the company, would, if it were not replaced by a similar sum, create considerable difficulty for the company on which the reclaimer's ability to make his livelihood depends, and that he therefore could not reasonably be expected to take this step if it were required to provide the respondent with an equal share. The same applies to sale by the reclaimer of his shares: it is by virtue of his major shareholding as well as of his position as director, that the reclaimer's ability to run the company depends. If withdrawal of the loan without replacing it with a similar amount of working capital, or if a sale of the reclaimer's shares were the only means of achieving an equal division of property, I would be in no doubt that an equal division would not be justified at least to the extent sought by the reclaimer in this motion, i.e. by reducing to nil the £50,000 which the Lord Ordinary found to be due by him on the assumption that he also paid off the respondent's share of the mortgage debt secured over Almond Lodge, the former matrimonial home, in which the respondent continues to reside.

But it is clear from the evidence that the order for equal sharing pronounced by the Lord Ordinary does not require either that the working capital of the company should be reduced, or that such capital should be replaced by bank borrowing (which is contrary to the policy of the company adopted for reasons which seem to me entirely reasonable), or that the reclaimer's shareholding should be realised. I understood it to be conceded by the reclaimer's senior counsel that a sum could be raised by the company without undue difficulty, by borrowing on the security of certain premises in Glasgow. That sum would be sufficient to enable the reclaimer and his fellow director, Mr Low, to withdraw pro rata part of the loans which they had made to the company. In the reclaimer's case this withdrawal would amount to £90,000 which would be sufficient to allow him to pay off the respondent's half share of the mortgage debt, and to pay the £50,000. Further at the date of separation, which in my opinion is the date on which the "use made of" matrimonial property primarily fails to be assessed, the reclaimer held certain sums on account, including one of £276,636 on deposit account which he intended to devote to the purchase of an alternative place to live, and which he has since used for that purpose. In my opinion the "use made of" that sum at the date of separation includes use as a means of holding funds earmarked for the purchase of a house. It would be illogical to regard the whole of that sum as being freely available for distribution simply because the reclaimer purchased alternative accommodation after rather than before he moved out of the matrimonial home.

Nevertheless it was a sum which could have been easily realised at the date of separation and if only a small part of it were required for the purpose of achieving an equal division, it should not be ignored in considering whether departure from equal sharing is justified.

During the course of the submission by junior counsel for the respondent it was suggested that in a situation where matrimonial property is such that an equal division in value can be achieved without realisation of an item or items which could not be reasonably expected to be realised or divided or used as security, subs 6(d) has no application. Difficulty of realisation is not, of course, the only circumstance referred to in the paragraph, but, even if it were, I would not have agreed with this submission. The existence of other resources from which an order for equal sharing involving payment can be easily met is plainly a very material consideration when it comes to determining whether departure from equal division is justified by any difficulty of realising a particular asset; *Little v Little,* per Lord President, in relation to the division of pension benefits, at 788L-789A. But it is not conclusive, since it is the nature of the whole of the matrimonial property and the extent to which that whole can be realised which has to be considered, not just a particular part of it. It is not difficult to envisage circumstances in which an order for equal division in value might leave one party with assets which were for practical purposes unrealisable for example the former matrimonial home, the other party being awarded a preponderance of cash or other easily realisable assets. In such circumstances, and perhaps also in others, there might be special circumstances justifying an order for sharing in proportions which were unequal in value, notwithstanding that an order for equal division could be complied with without realisation of that part of the property which was difficult to realise. I therefore agree with the reclaimer's submission that it is relevant to consider whether an order for equal sharing in value would lead to a marked disparity in the nature of the property allocated, and if so, whether that disparity is such as to justify departure from the principle of equal division.

But on a consideration of all the assets allocated to each party in the present case, I do not consider that any such disparity justifies departure from the principle. The resources which the reclaimer would find difficult to realise are those which assist in providing him with a substantial, income. The respondent on the other hand will have to rely for income to a large extent on income derived from realisation and investment of assets which are allocated to her, particularly from realisation of the "development site" which forms part of the area in which the matrimonial home is situated, and from the £50,000 which the Lord Ordinary found to be due to her. On this account I see no unfairness resulting from the fact that the order pronounced by the Lord Ordinary involves the transfer to her of cash and of a readily realisable asset amounting to sums which are not freely available to the reclaimer. I recognise that there will be disparity between the position of the reclaimer and that of the respondent as regards the nature of the property allocated to each of them. Some such disparity is inevitable in this and no doubt in virtually all other cases. In my opinion it is not in the present case one which justifies departure from the principle of equal sharing.

On behalf of the reclaimer it was also submitted that the order for equal sharing was not, as is provided for in s 8(2)(b) of the Act, "reasonable having regard to the resources of the parties".

But although this requirement is expressed as additional to the principles which relate to the sharing of matrimonial property expressed in sections 9 and 10, in the present case the factual basis on which the argument was advanced appears to me to be identical to that on which it was contended that there were special circumstances justifying unequal division. In my opinion it is clear that the reclaimer's resources are sufficient to enable him to meet an order for equal sharing without undue difficulty, and that such an order is reasonable in this regard.

In respect of periodical allowance the Lord Ordinary stated that he had regard to the capital which he was proposing to award to the appellant, and it is clearly correct that this should be done. By virtue of s 8(2)(a) of the Act any order, including one for periodical allowance, must be justified by the principles set out in s 9, and one of these principles, provided for in s 9(1)(d) is that: "a party who has been dependent to a substantial degree on the financial support of the other party should be awarded such financial provision as is reasonable to enable him to adjust, over a period of not more than three years from the date of the decree of divorce, to the loss of support on divorce".

The Lord Ordinary awarded periodical allowance for that maximum period, but it is not clear why he did so in view of the fact that part of the capital which he was awarding to the respondent *i.e.* "the development site", was obviously intended by the reclaimer to provide the respondent with an asset which could easily be realised and which would yield a substantial income, additional to that which she would receive from the £50,000. In that respect the opportunity over a period of three years afforded to the pursuer to "consider her future arrangements" appears to me to be unnecessarily long. I agree with your Lordship that a period of six months would be sufficient to enable the respondent to realise the development site if that is what she wishes to do, and that if she did so the loss of support referred to in s 9(1)(d) would not be such as to justify any additional award after that period has expired. It would not be reasonable for the respondent to delay realising the site at the appellant's expense. I also agree that, for the reduced period of six months during which the allowance will be paid, there is insufficient justification to disturb the amount awarded by the Lord Ordinary. For these reasons I agree that the reclaiming motion should be dealt with as your Lordship proposes.

Counsel for Pursuer and Respondent, M.C.N. Scott, Q.C., Macnair; Solicitors, Brodies, WS—Counsel for Defender and Reclaimer, Stewart, Q.C., Wise; Solicitors, Morton Fraser Milligan.

JACKSON v. JACKSON

Outer House, July 28, 1999. Reported 1999 Fam.L.R. 108.

OPINION OF LORD MACFADYEN

In this action of divorce the contentious issues relate to the parties' respective conclusions for financial provision.

Divorce

The ground on which the pursuer seeks decree of divorce is that the marriage has broken down irretrievably by reason of the defender's behaviour. The defender did not seek to resist the granting of decree of divorce on that ground. The pursuer gave evidence in support of her averments about the defender's behaviour, and corroborative evidence was provided, in affidavit form, by the pursuer's son, David Nisbet. I am satisfied by that evidence that the marriage has broken down irretrievably. I shall therefore grant decree of divorce.

Financial Claims

The pursuer concludes for (1) a capital sum of £300,000, (2) a periodical allowance of £400 per week, (3) a property transfer order in her favour in respect of the defender's half share in the former matrimonial home at 387 Queensferry Road, Edinburgh, and (4) an order for sale of both parties' shares in a company called P&B Enterprises Limited ("P&B") and for division of the whole free proceeds thereof, under deduction of expenses of sale and capital gains tax (CGT), equally between the parties. At the outset of the proof, leave was sought and granted to amend the defender's conclusions. As so amended, they are for (1) a property transfer order in his favour in respect of all or part of the pursuer's holding of shares in P&B, and (2) a capital sum of £150,000. In his submissions at the conclusion of the proof counsel for the pursuer did not maintain the claim for a periodical allowance; maintained the claim for a capital sum, albeit for a lesser amount; maintained the claim for a property transfer order in respect of the house; advanced (without any conclusion to found it) a claim for a property transfer order in respect of contents of the house; and restricted the order sought in respect of the shares in P&B to one for sale of the whole shares, leaving the free proceeds to be divided in accordance with the parties' shareholdings, and leaving each party to bear his or her own CGT liability. Counsel for the defender invited me to refuse the pursuer's claims for a capital sum and for property transfer orders. She did not maintain the defender's claim for a property transfer order in respect of the shares in P&B. She did not oppose the making of an order for the sale of the shares in P&B, but submitted that the sale should be postponed for three years. She sought, finally, a capital sum in favour of the defender of the amount concluded for, postponed until the sale of the shares was effected.

The order which I make for financial provision must, in terms of s. 8(2) of the Family Law (Scotland) Act 1985 ("the 1985 Act"), be (a) justified by the principles set out in s. 9, and (b) reasonable having regard to the resources of the parties. Both counsel sought in their submissions to rely on the principle set out in s. 9(1)(a), namely that the net value of the matrimonial property should be shared fairly between the parties. Counsel for the pursuer also sought to rely on the presumption set out in s. 10(1) that equal sharing is fair sharing. Counsel for the defender on the other hand sought to argue that there were special circumstances which justified unequal sharing. She also sought to rely on the principle set out in s. 9(1)(b), namely that fair account should be taken of any economic advantage derived by one party from contributions by the other.

Matrimonial Property

Since both parties rely on s. 9(1)(a), it is necessary to ascertain the net value of the matrimonial property at the relevant date. It was a matter of agreement that the relevant date was October 17, 1996, the date of service of the summons (s 10(3)(b)).

(a) Agreed Items

The identity and value of many items of matrimonial property were agreed in a joint minute. It is convenient to set out the agreed items at this stage, since nothing more will then require to be said about them until they are brought into account in the final determination of the orders to be made.

TABLE 1

Item of Matrimonial Property	Pursuer	Defender
House at 387 Queensferry Road	72,500.00	72,500.00
Fidelity personal equity plans (PEPs)	14,641.00	11,689.00
M & G PEPs	7,158.00	8,599.00
Provident Mutual personal pension plans	27,206.00	100,731.00
Scottish Amicable personal pension plan	25,354.00	
Standard Life life policy	1,143.00	
United Friendly life policy	658.00	
State Farm life policy LF#1369-07	600.00	
State Farm life policy 4193849	2,665.00	
State Farm life policy 5175622	2197.00	
Australian Mutual Provident life policy (part)	931.00	
Scottish Power plc shares	7,000.00	7,000.00
Royal Bank of Scotland plc account	1,384.00	
Clydesdale Bank account	31,500.00	
Texas Commerce Bank account		640.00
Totals	**£163,190.00**	**£232,906.00**

It was also agreed that at the relevant date the following debts, which fell to be brought into account, in terms of s. 10(2) of the 1985 Act, in calculating the net value of the matrimonial property, and which were all subsequently cleared by the defender, were outstanding:

TABLE 2

Debt	Amount
Bank of Scotland overdraft	£19,692.00
John Lewis account	659.00
Visa account	1,697.00
British Telecom account	66.00
British Gas account	125.00
Scottish Power account	96.00
Total	**£22,335.00**

It was also matter of agreement that at the relevant date the pursuer and the defender held 677,000 and 684,300 shares respectively in P&B. The history and valuation of those shares will require to be discussed in more detail. In addition, both parties had, at the relevant date, pension rights arising from their former employment with one or another of the companies in a group which it is convenient at this stage to call SOFEC. Again, the value of those rights was the subject of evidence and will require to be discussed in more detail. The other items of property about which evidence was led were certain jewellery and certain of the contents of the matrimonial home. There were also one or two debts which were not agreed.

(b) Jewellery
The jewellery in question was purchased by the defender for the pursuer in the course of the marriage. There was no dispute that it should remain in the hands of the pursuer. The only issue was as to the value at which it ought to be brought into account. Two experts gave evidence about its valuation. One thing that is clear is that its value in the pursuer's hands is substantially less than the aggregate of the sums spent by the defender in acquiring it. It was not disputed, however, that it was its second hand value at the relevant date that fell to be brought into account. Counsel for the pursuer submitted that I should find that the value of the jewellery was £10,448. Counsel for the defender, on the other hand, suggested £13,381. Counsel for the pursuer's figure was based upon the valuation prepared on the instructions of the defender by John Whyte & Son Ltd (no 22/6 of process) and spoken to in evidence by their Mr Taylor. That valuation included the valuation of one particular diamond ring at £6,000. The other valuation that was put in evidence was by Goodwin's Antiques Ltd (no 19/6 of process) on the instructions of the pursuer and was spoken to by Mr Benjamin Goodwin. It brought out a total of £8,200, of which only £1,500 was attributed to the diamond ring, but otherwise reflected higher values per item than the Whytes report. It also omitted certain items included in the Whytes valuation. Counsel for the pursuer was content simply to accept the higher and more comprehensive valuation. Counsel for the defender, however, sought to justify the higher figure which she put forward by an eclectic approach to the two valuations. She submitted that the markedly higher value assigned to the diamond ring by Whytes should be accepted, and that the Whytes valuation for the items omitted from the Goodwins report should be included, but that

71

for the rest, the higher values found in the Goodwins report should be accepted. Counsel for the pursuer submitted that it was inappropriate to carry out such "cherry-picking". I accept counsel's submission on that point. I must form a view on the basis of conflicting expert evidence. There did not seem to me to be any basis in the evidence for regarding one expert as clearly right and the other clearly wrong. I must therefore take a broad view. But for Mr Taylor's clear evidence that he would recommend his employers to pay £6,000 for the diamond ring, I would have been inclined simply to average the two valuations. In light of that evidence, however, counsel for the pursuer's concession was in my view reasonable, and I shall adopt the value of £10,448.

(c) Contents of Matrimonial Home
An inventory and valuation of contents of the matrimonial home was prepared by Phillips Scotland (no 22/5 of process). The total value brought out as at the relevant date was £10,240. There were certain items which the defender wished to retain (items 13, 15, 19 and 21), the aggregate value of which appears to be £780. The defender accepted that the pursuer should have the remainder (the value of which was thus £9,460), although counsel for the defender suggested that it was unnecessary to pronounce a property transfer order to give effect to that allocation. Since the parties are broadly agreed on these matters, it seems to me to be appropriate to anticipate the agreed allocation and thus to bring the contents of the house into the account of matrimonial property on the footing that its value is £10,240 shared between the parties in the proportion of £9,460 to the pursuer and £780 to the defender.

(d) SOFEC Pensions
Both parties are entitled to pensions in respect of their former employment with SOFEC. There is no dispute as to the value of the pursuer's SOFEC pension. Parties are agreed that it should be brought into account at £6,039. There is, however, wide divergence as to the proper value to be attributed to the defender's SOFEC pension. The pursuer contends that the appropriate figure is £51,744, whereas the defender argues for £18,113.

The foundation of the defender's pension entitlement is to be found in a transaction which took place in 1993. The defender was, at that time, one of the shareholders in SOFEC Holdings Inc. The defender first worked for SOFEC Inc under contract in 1972. He became an employee of and stockholder in SOFEC in 1975. The company was sold to Vickers in 1982, but there followed a management buyout in 1988, which restored the defender to the position of being a stockholder. By that stage the group structure involved SOFEC Holdings Inc as the parent company and SOFEC Inc and SOFEC Ltd as subsidiaries. In 1993 the defender and his fellow stockholders sold their stock in SOFEC Holdings Inc to FMC Corporation. The purchase agreement between FMC Corporation and the defender and his fellow stockholders is no 21/15 of process. Annexed to it (no 21/18 of process) was a special fixed term employment agreement which was entered into between SOFEC Inc and the defender. Clause 1.06 of the latter agreement provided *inter alia* as follows: "Upon the execution of this Agreement FMC shall immediately vest EMPLOYEE [i.e. the defender] in a retirement benefit under its FMC Salaried Employees Retirement Plan by crediting EMPLOYEE with all past service with COMPANY [i.e. SOFEC Inc]. Such service shall count only for vesting under such plan. However, if Employee remains an employee of COMPANY or FMC or any affiliate of FMC continuously during the full term of this Agreement [i.e. until June 30, 1998], or if his employment is terminated by reason of his death or disability, he will also be credited with past service with COMPANY for calculation of benefit. If EMPLOYEE's employment is terminated [otherwise before its full term] he will be credited for 50 per cent of past service with the COMPANY for calculation of benefits."

In the event the defender remained in the employment of SOFEC Inc for the full term of the agreement. His pension entitlement will accordingly be calculated as if he had been in reckonable employment throughout his employment with SOFEC, *i.e.* since 1975. If, however, he had left the employment of SOFEC Inc at the relevant date, *i.e.* on October 17, 1996, his pension would have been calculated on the basis that he would be credited with only 50 per cent of that total service.

The defender's valuation figure was explained in evidence by Mr Kenneth Auld, an actuary. He proceeded on the basis of information from Hewitt Associates, FMC's actuaries, which is contained in no 29/1 of process. Their calculation proceeded on the basis of taking into account only the portion of the benefit attributable to the period of service between the date of marriage and the relevant date, and on the basis that only 50 per cent of that service should be credited because the relevant date was before the expiry of the full term of the employment agreement. Mr Auld adjusted Hewitt Associates' figure to allow for valuation at the relevant date, and converted the result to sterling, yielding the figure of £18,113. The pursuer's valuation figure was spoken to by Mr T F Marshall, also an actuary. He considered that the Hewitts figure should be adjusted to correct the effect of their having proceeded on what he regarded as the unrealistic basis of a weighted male/female mortality table. They did that, he understood, because of the impact of American legislation, but he maintained that British actuarial practice recognised the reality of different mortality rates for males and females. Apart from that point, his conclusion differed from Mr Auld's because he treated the whole pension entitlement as referable to the period of the marriage, and did not make the 50 per cent discount derived from the fact that the relevant date was before the expiry of the full term of the employment agreement.

Apart from Mr Marshall's point about mortality tables, which I accept as sound, the issue of valuation of the defender's pension entitlement depends not on actuarial issues, but on questions of law. Before attempting to answer those questions it is convenient to note the terms of the relevant legislation. [His Lordship narrated the terms of section 10(5) of the 1985 Act and continued:]

Section 10(10) defines "benefits under a pension scheme" as including any benefits by way of pension, whether under a pension scheme (as defined in the subsection) or not. I did not understand it to be disputed that the defender's benefits under the FMC retirement plan were "benefits under a pension scheme" in the statutory sense. The other potentially relevant provisions are those of the Divorce etc (Pensions) (Scotland) Regulations 1996 ("the 1996 Regulations"). [His Lordship narrated the terms of reg 3 and proceeded:]

There then follow three subparagraphs dealing with identified categories of pension scheme, all making reference to the value of the cash equivalent to which the party would have been entitled if the pensionable service had terminated on the relevant date. It was common ground that none of those provisions was applicable to an overseas pension such as the defender's benefit under the FMC retirement plan. The applicable provision is accordingly subpara (d) which is in the following terms: "where any benefits which a party has or may have under a pension scheme as at the relevant date are not valued in accordance with subparagraphs (a), (b) or (c) above, their value, as at that date, shall be such as may be calculated by the court by such method as it shall see fit."

In light of those provisions the first question which arises is what portion of the defender's rights or interests in the benefit under the FMC retirement plan is referable to the period between the date of the marriage and the relevant date. In short, counsel for the pursuer's submission was that since the whole benefits arose out of a contract entered into in 1993, *i.e.* after the marriage and before the relevant date, what fell to be brought into account as part of the matrimonial property was the whole value at the relevant date of the defender's rights and interests in the FMC retirement plan. He sought support for that submission in part in the terms of reg. 3(3) of the 1996 Regulations where, in laying down the formula for calculation of the proportion of benefits to be brought into account as matrimonial property as A x B ¼ C, A is defined as the value of the rights or interests in the benefits at the relevant date, B is defined as the period of C which falls within the period of the marriage before the relevant date, and C is defined as "the period of the membership ... in the pension scheme before the relevant date". He pointed out that the fact that the defender had been given credit for years of service with SOFEC prior to 1993 did not alter the fact that the period of his membership of the scheme began in 1993. Applying the statutory formula, all of period C fell within the period of the marriage. He also, in order to counter an argument advanced by counsel for the defender on the basis that a pension was to be regarded as deferred pay, characterised the defender's enhanced entitlement under the FMC retirement plan as deferred consideration for the purchase of his stock in SOFEC Holdings Inc.

Counsel for the defender's submission was that there was no reason to depart from the normal view that a pension was deferred pay. The defender would not have been given the enhanced benefit that he was given if he had not been in the service of SOFEC from 1975. The point could be tested by looking at the fact that each stockholder was given enhanced pension entitlement by reference to the period of his individual service with SOFEC. It should therefore be seen as a recognition of the contribution which the defender's past service had made to the value of SOFEC at the date of acquisition. It was properly to be regarded as deferred pay for that service. The period to which the defender's rights or interests in the benefit under the FMC retirement plan were referable was thus the whole period since 1975, part of which was before the marriage. Their value therefore fell to be apportioned, and the proportion attributable to the credited years before 1986 left out of the valuation of matrimonial property. In relation to the argument based on reg 3(3), counsel for the defender submitted that the regulations were subordinate to the statute, and that in order to reconcile reg 3(3) with s. 10(5), the reference to a party's period of membership of the pension scheme should be read as wide enough to include not only actual membership but also credited membership.

In my view the question which I must determine is whether the whole or only part of the defender's rights and interests in the benefits under the FMC retirement plan are "referable" to the period of the marriage prior to the relevant date. In the first place, it seems to me that no conclusive answer to that question is provided by examining the word "referable". There is a sense in which a part of the defender's rights is "referable" to the period before 1986, and there is a sense in which no part of them is so "referable". I do, however, derive some assistance from the general scheme of s. 10 in its approach to the identification and valuation of matrimonial property, and in particular the reference in s. 10(4) to acquisition during the marriage but before the relevant date. It seems to me that the general approach is (subject to the exception of the matrimonial home and its contents) to leave out of account that which is acquired before the marriage, and to bring into account (subject to the exception for gifts and inheritance) that which is acquired thereafter. In the special case of pension rights, because of their nature, language other than reference to acquisition is required. It seems to me that the use of the word "referable" is intended to secure that there is not brought into account as matrimonial property any part of the pension rights which the party can be regarded as already "having" at the date of the marriage. Secondly, although it is no doubt right that a pension is ordinarily to be regarded as deferred remuneration, the particular circumstances of the present case in my view support the alternative analysis suggested by counsel for the pursuer. It seems to me to be clear that as at 1993 the defender had no subsisting pension rights attributable to his employment with SOFEC. The pension rights conferred on him at that stage were, in reality, part of a package of consideration for the acquisition of his interest in SOFEC. It was no doubt convenient to the defender to have part of the consideration structured as an enhanced pension. But it does not seem to me that it is appropriate to carry the effect of that structuring to the extent of treating as a benefit already in part subsisting at the date of the marriage a pension which first came into existence in 1993. Thirdly, the language used in reg 3(3) in my view affords strong support for the conclusion that "referable" in s. 10(5) should be construed in the way which I propose. It tends to confirm that an interest in a pension is referable to the period before marriage to the extent that it arises out of membership of the scheme before marriage. Here there was no period of pre-marriage membership. For these reasons, I conclude that the whole of the defender's interest in the FMC retirement scheme as at the relevant date falls to be brought into account as matrimonial property.

The second question which arises is whether in valuing that interest at the relevant date the effect of the terms of clause 1.06 of the employment agreement is that account should only be taken of 50 per cent of the credited years. If the valuation had been being carried out under subpara (a), (b) or (c) of reg 3(2), the answer would, it seems to me, have been in the affirmative, because on a notional termination of pensionable service on the relevant date the cash equivalent to which the defender would have been entitled on that date would have reflected the reduction to 50 per cent imposed in the event of early termination. Under subpara (d), however, the method of calculation is left to my discretion. Counsel for the pursuer referred to *Bannon v. Bannon*, 1993 S.L.T. 999 at 1003-1004, and submitted that I should not shut my eyes to the events which are known to have happened. The defender did in fact complete the whole period of service required to qualify for the full pension based on 100 per cent of the credited years. Any assessment made at the relevant date of the likelihood of his doing so would have led to the conclusion that in all probability he would do so. It was plainly to his advantage to do so. Counsel for the defender submitted that I should exercise my discretion under subpara. (d) in such a way as to approximate to the result which would have followed from the application of any of the other subparagraphs. It seems to me, however, that I should adopt the approach which yields the most realistic view of the value of the defender's interest in the pension scheme at the relevant date. I find it instructive that Mr Auld said in evidence that, if he had not thought himself constrained by the regulations, he would not have made the 50 per cent discount. That seems to me to indicate that he would have regarded the full valuation as reasonable in those circumstances. That is my view too.

For all these reasons, I am of opinion that the proper value to be attributed at the relevant date to that portion of the defender's SOFEC pension which falls to be brought into account as matrimonial property is £51,744.

(e) Shareholdings in P&B

P&B was incorporated on July 19, 1995. It owns and operates the Rowardennan Hotel, along with associated chalet letting, boat hire and ferry operating enterprises. The share capital of the company is divided into 1,500,000 shares of £1 each, of which 1,361,300 shares are issued and fully paid. Of the issued shares, the defender holds 684,300 (50.27 per cent) and the pursuer holds 677,000 (49.73 per cent). The parties' shareholdings were valued by Michael J. Gilbert of Scott Oswald CA, whose report is no 28/1 of process, and who gave evidence. He valued the entire shareholding in P&B on a going concern basis at the relevant date at the sum of £899,639. Since both parties adopted that valuation as the basis for their submissions, it is unnecessary for me to examine the detail of the material that led Mr Gilbert to that conclusion. It was in their approach to the assessment of the value of the parties' individual shareholdings at the relevant date that parties differed.

As a matter of arithmetic, 49.73 per cent of £899,639 is £447,390. In paragraph 4.2 of his report, Mr Gilbert applied a discount to that sum in order to assess the value of the pursuer's shareholding in P&B. He explained that that discount was necessary to reflect the fact that the pursuer's holding is a minority one, albeit a minority of sufficient size to block the passing of a special resolution. He also expressed the view that since the company had, at the relevant date, only recently commenced trading the value of the minority shareholding should reflect the underlying net assets. In view of those considerations, he suggested a discount of 30 per cent. The application of that discount brings the value of the pursuer's shareholding down to £313,173. Correspondingly, 50.27 per cent of £899,639 is £452,249, but in cross examination Mr Gilbert accepted that if the holdings were being valued individually the value of the defender's holding also required to be discounted to reflect the fact that the pursuer could block a special resolution. He suggested a discount of 5 per cent on that account. That would reduce the value of the defender's holding to £429,636. In his submissions counsel for the pursuer adopted those discounted figures as the values at which the parties' respective shareholdings should enter the computation of matrimonial property.

Counsel for the defender on the other hand submitted that in the circumstances it was inappropriate to apply the discounts which Mr Gilbert proposed. Essentially, her point was that such discounts were appropriate if one was valuing the interest of an individual shareholder, but not if one was valuing the entire shareholding in the company. It was appropriate to adopt a realistic approach to matters of valuation *(Savage v. Savage; Brown v. Brown, McConnell v. McConnell)*. Here it was common ground that it was going to be necessary in practical terms either (i) to sell the company as a whole, or (ii) to sell the business of the company as a going concern, and then wind the company up. In either of those situations, the whole value of the company would be realised, and divided between the parties in proportion to their respective shareholdings. There was therefore no need for the discounts suggested. What was necessary was an allowance for the expenses of sale, and Mr Gilbert estimated those in evidence at 2.5 per cent. Making that allowance, the net value of the defender's shareholding at the relevant date was £440,942, and that of the pursuer's shareholding £436,205.

In my view counsel for the defender's submissions on this point are sound. As I understood him, Mr Gilbert said in evidence in chief that the discounts which he proposed were not appropriate in a context in which the whole company was being sold. Since it is common ground that that, or its equivalent, is the course which should be followed in the present case, I do not consider that it would be appropriate to include both parties' interests in the company in the computation of matrimonial property on an artificial basis which would not be reflected in the events which are going to happen. To do so would introduce an appearance of much greater inequality in the way in which the matrimonial property is held than is truly present.

(f) Debts

In addition to the agreed items set out in Table 2, there was evidence of two further debts which, it was said, the defender had discharged. One was a Marks & Spencers account for £265. The other was a sum of £932 said to have been paid by the defender after the relevant date in discharge of an income tax liability of the pursuer for the year 1995-96.

Counsel for the pursuer's position was that only the Bank of Scotland overdraft should be brought into account in diminution of the net total of matrimonial property. The other debts should be treated as ongoing alimentary payment by the defender in support of the pursuer which did not affect the capital position. Counsel for the defender submitted that there was no statutory justification for that approach. Although the matter is almost de minimis, I prefer counsel for the defender's submission.

On the question whether the tax payment should be treated as a matrimonial debt, counsel for the defender referred to *McConnell v. McConnell*, 1997 Fam. L.R. 97 per Lord Osborne at paragraph 19-56; *Buchan v. Buchan*; *MacRitchie v. MacRitchie*; and *McCormick v. McCormick*, 1994 S.C.L.R. 958, *per* Lord Marnoch at 959-960. Since the value of the point is small in the present case, I do not propose to discuss it at length. I prefer the view adopted in the first three cases to that adopted by Lord Marnoch in *McCormick*. I therefore consider that the tax debt subsequently paid by the defender should be taken into account as a deduction in the computation of matrimonial property. Since the defender bore the whole amount of the matrimonial debts, I regard it as appropriate that they should be deducted in whole from his assets.

(g) Total of Agreed and Disputed Items

I can now return to my computation of the value of the net matrimonial property at the relevant date, bringing together the agreed figures from Tables 1 and 2, and my decisions on the disputed items.

TABLE 3

Item	Pursuer	Defender
Agreed items per Table 1	163,190.00	232,906.00
Jewellery	10,448.00	
Contents of matrimonial home	9,460.00	780.00
SOFEC pensions	6,039.00	51,744.00
Shareholdings in P&B	436,205.00	440,942.00
Totals (property)	**£625,342.00**	**£726,372.00**
Agreed debts per Table 2		£22,335.00
Additional debts		1197.00
Total (debts)		£23,532.00
Total Net Matrimonial Property	**£625,342.00**	**£702,840.00**

Fair Sharing

The principle set out in s. 9(1)(a) of the 1985 Act is that the net value of the matrimonial property should be shared fairly between the parties. Section 10(1) provides that the net value shall be taken to be shared fairly when it is shared equally or in such other proportions as are justified by special circumstances. There is thus a presumption in favour of equal sharing, which may be displaced if special circumstances exist which justify some other proportion (*Jacques v. Jacques*, 1997 S.C., HL 20, per Lord Clyde at 24). [His Lordship narrated the terms of section 10(6)(a), (b) and (d) and proceeded:]

As was confirmed in *Jacques,* those provisions are illustrative only, and the presence of circumstances of the sort mentioned in one or more of the illustrations does not necessarily justify unequal sharing.

Counsel for the defender submitted that in the present case there were special circumstances which justified unequal sharing. She submitted that the inequality that was justified was the allocation of at least 60 per cent of the matrimonial property to the defender, with the balance to the pursuer. She also submitted that the same result was justified by the application of the principle set out in s. 9(1)(b) of the 1985 Act, but I shall return to that aspect of her submissions later.

The circumstances which she submitted were special, and justified the unequal division for which she argued, were those surrounding the derivation of a substantial part of the parties' wealth from the defender's previous involvement with SOFEC. Approximately two thirds of the total of the net value of the matrimonial property at the relevant date is attributable to the shareholdings in P&B. The source of the funds used to purchase P&B was the price received for the sale of the defender's interest in SOFEC. The defender had been associated with SOFEC since 1972. He had been an employee since 1975. He had been a stockholder prior to the sale to Vickers in 1982. He had been involved with SOFEC for 14 years before the marriage. He had been involved in the development of the company in a highly specialised field of engineering in relation to the offshore oil industry. He had become a stockholder again in 1988 at the time of the management buyout. The price which he paid to reacquire his stockholding (£15,000) was of no real importance. What was significant was his long involvement in the company before the marriage, and the substantial contribution which he made, through his expertise and hard work, to its development. When FMC acquired SOFEC, the consideration which was paid was not simply for the stock, but to a material extent for the defender's knowhow, his covenant not to compete with SOFEC, and the indemnities into which he entered. Counsel for the defender did not identify particular proportions, but the defender avers (and the figures for knowhow and the covenant are borne out in exhibits E and F to the purchase agreement) that the price for the shares was $1,083,321, for the knowhow $360,000 and for the covenant $715,232. To a material extent, therefore, it was submitted, the funds realised in 1993 were derived from the defender's efforts prior to the marriage. If it had not been for his earlier involvement the opportunity to realise the wealth that was realised in 1993 would not have arisen.

Counsel for the defender sought to minimise the importance of the fact that the shareholding in P&B was taken approximately equally between the parties. It is, however, in my view necessary to note the sequence of events which followed the sale of the defender's interest in SOFEC. Understandably, he wished to minimise so far as he legitimately could his liability to

CGT. It was in order to obtain rollover relief that a large part of the proceeds of sale was invested in P&B. A claim was also made for retirement relief in the pursuer's name. The argument on which that claim was based depended on the proposition that half of the stockholding in SOFEC belonged to the pursuer. The defender said in evidence that he regarded the stock as belonging to him and the pursuer jointly because they were married. It is, to my mind, reasonably clear from the purchase agreement that as a matter of law the defender alone was the stockholder. Clause 1 of the purchase agreement provided that the stockholders' spouses would join in the execution of the share transfers "so as to release and convey any community property interest they or any of them may have in the Shares", and the pursuer did indeed sign the share transfers in pursuance of that provision. The parties were, however, then resident in Scotland, and were not subject to any American community of property regime. The terms of the purchase agreement were disclosed to the Inland Revenue, and there was also produced to them a letter from the company secretary of SOFEC (No. 34/3b of process) stating, "As Mr Jackson's spouse, Mrs Jackson owned one-half of the shares." Whether that was a misunderstanding of the position or not, the Inland Revenue accepted the claim for retirement relief in the pursuer's name. The consequence of that way of presenting the matter to the Inland Revenue was that, to obtain rollover relief, the reinvestment also had to be a joint one. It seems to me, however, that on the evidence which the defender gave before me, it would be wrong to regard the fact that the investment in P&B was made in name of both parties as merely a device to minimise tax liability. The defender, as I have already recorded, said that he regarded the stockholding in SOFEC as being joint property because he and the pursuer were married. Whether that was correct or not as a matter of law, it is in my view an indication which I can accept of the way in which the defender viewed the matter. Earlier in his evidence, in relation to the shares in P&B, the defender said that he wished the pursuer to have them. I accept that, too, as an accurate reflection of the way he was thinking at the time.

Counsel for the pursuer submitted that there were no special circumstances which justified unequal sharing of the matrimonial property, still less aggravating the existing inequality. The mere fact that assets derived from the defender's success in business did not justify unequal division. The stockholding in SOFEC which was sold in 1993 had been acquired during the marriage, in 1988, for £15,000. Such evidence as the defender gave about funding the purchase by a loan repaid out of deferred income which arose in respect of a period before the marriage should not be accepted without vouching. In any event the value of the stock had plainly increased greatly during the marriage, and in that context the source of funding of the purchase was of little significance. Counsel for the pursuer founded on the way ownership of the SOFEC stock had been represented to the Inland Revenue, and on the fact that, whatever the ownership of that stock had been, the shareholding in P&B had been taken in approximately equal shares. The defender's agreement to that allocation of shareholding was a very strong factor weighing against unequal division. Although s. 10(6)(a) addressed the question of the relevance of an agreement as a special circumstance supporting unequal division, it was clear from what Lord Clyde said in *Jacques* at 25 that it was legitimate to have regard to an agreement to share an asset equally in considering whether equal sharing or some other proportion would be fair. Counsel for the pursuer also submitted that it was relevant to bear in mind that the pursuer would require to live in part on income from her capital for the rest of her life, since she had no realistic prospects of future employment, whereas the defender was still of working age, and the restrictive covenant which prevented him from currently deploying his professional expertise would expire in June 2000. Although the pursuer had her pensions, they were not large. She had had to use some of the capital she had at the relevant date to live on in the interval since then, which was at least in part attributable to the fact that the defender had been less than frank in disclosing his income to the court in the context of the pursuer's motion for interim aliment. In all the circumstances the presumption in favour of equal sharing of the matrimonial property had not been displaced.

In my opinion, the evidence did not disclose special circumstances which displace the presumption that equal sharing of the value of the matrimonial property is fair. I accept that the source of the funds used to acquire a substantial part of the matrimonial property, namely the parties' shareholdings in P&B, was the sum of money received by the defender in respect of the acquisition by FMC of his interest in SOFEC. I accept that to some extent those funds may be regarded as not "derived from the ... efforts of the parties during the marriage" (s 10(6)(b)). It does not seem to me, however, that the evidence very clearly established to what extent those funds were, and to what extent they were not, so derived. It is right that the defender was involved in SOFEC from 1972, and as an employee and stockholder from 1975. He sold his stockholding to Vickers in 1982, however, and therefore his position at the date of the marriage was that he was simply an employee, albeit a senior and no doubt important employee, of a company owned by a substantial international group. He reacquired a proprietary interest in SOFEC, now in the form of SOFEC Holdings Inc, in the management buyout of 1988. The price which he paid to acquire that interest was £15,000. I did not find the evidence about how he funded that purchase very clear. It may be that it was in some way funded from income from the period before the marriage. But counsel for the defender did not seek to lay very much stress on that factor. It is no doubt simplistic to compare the 1988 purchase price of £15,000 with the 1993 sale consideration, whether the price of the stock itself ($1,083,321) or the aggregate consideration ($1,083,321 + $360,000 + $715,232 = $2,158,553). It is not, I think, on that basis possible to calculate the proportion of the 1993 price that may be regarded as derived from the defender's efforts before the marriage. The share price element of the 1993 transaction suggests, however, that there had been substantial growth in value between 1988 and 1993. To a material extent, it seems to me that that is likely to have reflected the defender's expertise and business acumen during the period of the marriage. There is no basis in the evidence on which I feel able to form a reliable view about the extent to which the knowhow payment reflects knowhow which the defender had already built up before the marriage. The payment for the restrictive covenant might be analysed in a number of ways. It might be regarded as a reflection of the skill and specialised knowledge which the defender had built up throughout his time with SOFEC, *i.e.* 11 years before the marriage and seven after it. It might, on the other hand be regarded as the price for the defender's agreement not to deploy that skill and knowledge in competition with FMC during the period 1993 to 2000, *i.e.* three years before the relevant date and four years after it. If those circumstances had stood alone, I would have found it very difficult to reach a conclusion as to whether they were of such a nature as to justify holding that the matrimonial property bought with the proceeds of the SOFEC sale should be divided otherwise than equally. There is, however, another aspect of the matter which, in my view, should be regarded as removing the difficulty. That aspect is not the way the defender dealt with the proceeds of the SOFEC sale in relation to his tax affairs. It is, rather, the fact that he chose to invest the sum realised from SOFEC in the purchase of a company, with the shares taken almost equally between him and the pursuer. I have already recorded that the defender said in evidence that that was done because he wished the pursuer to have the shares, and that I have accepted that evidence as a true reflection of his attitude at the time. I have also noted that that aspect of his evidence fitted in with his expressed attitude to the SOFEC stock, that he regarded it as belonging to them both because they were married. Section 10(6)(a) makes any agreement as to the division of matrimonial property a potential "special circumstance". Here I rely on the agreement (and, perhaps more importantly, on the underlying intention on the defender's part which it reflects) not in support of unequal division, but as countering the potential effect of other circumstances and reinforcing the presumption in favour of equality. I regard the passage in Lord Clyde's speech in *Jacques* at 25 as supporting the legitimacy of that approach. For those reasons I conclude that the presumption in favour of the fairness of equal sharing of the net value of the matrimonial property has not been displaced.

Economic Advantage or Disadvantage

Section 9(1)(b) of the 1985 Act sets out the principle that: "fair account should be taken of any economic advantage derived by either party from contributions by the other, and of any economic disadvantage suffered by either party in the interests of the other party or of the family".

Section 9(2) defines "economic advantage" as including gains in capital. Section 11(2) directs the court, in applying s. 9(1)(b), to have regard to the balance of economic advantage or disadvantage, and the extent to which any imbalance will be corrected by sharing matrimonial property or otherwise.

Counsel for the defender submitted that an alternative route to the result which she primarily sought to reach by way of special circumstances justifying unequal sharing of the value of the matrimonial property was by way of the application of the principle set out in s. 9(1)(b). She said that the pursuer had enjoyed an economic advantage in the form of gaining capital which had been contributed by the defender. It was, she said, an obvious case for applying the s. 9(1)(b) principle to the effect of restoring to the defender, the contributor, some of the capital which the pursuer had gained from him. She referred to *Loudon v. Loudon, De Winton v. De Winton*, and *Sinclair v. Sinclair*.

Counsel for the pursuer submitted that this aspect of counsel for the defender's submissions involved a misconstruction of the legislation. It was contrary to the scheme of the Act to take account of economic advantage derived by one party from the other in the form of capital which formed part of the matrimonial property. Section 9(1)(b) was aimed at circumstances which did not involve matrimonial property as such. An example of the proper application of the s. 9(1)(b) principle was to be found in *De Winton*, where the income contribution by the pursuer conferred on the defender an economic advantage in the preservation and enhancement of his non-matrimonial capital. The present case was clearly distinguishable from that.

It does not seem to me that the proper relationship between s. 9(1)(a) and s. 9(1)(b) has been fully worked out in the cases which were cited to me. In *Loudon* s. 9(1)(b) considerations appear to have been taken into account in determining the fair sharing of matrimonial property, but I am not convinced that that is a sound approach. I am inclined to think that the correct analysis in that case would have been that the s. 9(1)(a) principle dictated equal sharing of the value of matrimonial property, but that the s. 9(1)(b) principle then came into play as a separate justification for a different order for financial provision from the one which would have been justified if regard had been had only to s. 9(1)(a). There is no difficulty in applying s. 9(1)(b) where, as in *De Winton* and *Sinclair,* the economic advantage does not bear on matrimonial property. While I do not rule out the possibility that in some circumstances s. 9(1)(b) may be capable of being invoked where the economic advantage does bear on matrimonial property, it seems to me that there is a serious risk of undermining the s. 9(1)(a) principle, the presumption that equal sharing is fair, and the need for special circumstances to displace the presumption, if in any case in which a party fails to displace the presumption of equal sharing, the same ground can then be traversed again in the guise of applying the s. 9(1)(b) principle. Having held, as I have, that the presumption of equal sharing has not been displaced, it would in my view be a misuse of s. 9(1)(b) to review the sharing of matrimonial property by testing it in terms of taking fair account of economic advantage. I am therefore of opinion that counsel for the defender's alternative argument under s. 9(1)(b) is unsound.

Property Transfer or Capital Sum

As I noted at the beginning of this opinion, by the end of the proof the only claims for property transfer orders which were maintained were (i) the pursuer's claim in terms of the third conclusion for transfer to her of the defender's one half pro indiviso share of the former matrimonial home at 387 Queensferry Road, Edinburgh, and (ii) the pursuer's claim stated at the bar but not expressed in any conclusion for transfer of the greater part of the contents of the matrimonial home valued by Phillips Scotland. The pursuer also claimed a capital sum to effect equal sharing of the value of the matrimonial property. The defender also made a claim for a capital sum, but on the view that I have taken of what would constitute fair sharing, that does not now arise. The remaining issue is therefore in what form the equalising transfer of value in favour of the pursuer should be made.

It was not, as I understood the position, disputed that the defender should have certain identified items of the contents of the house, while the pursuer should have the balance. If parties are able to deal with that by agreement there is no need for a formal order. I have given effect to the division which seems to be agreed by anticipating that allocation of the contents in calculating the matrimonial property held by each party. If for any reason a formal order is thought to be required, an opportunity to deal with the necessary amendment of the pursuer's conclusions will arise when the case calls by order for the other purpose which I shall explain later.

So far as the matrimonial home is concerned, counsel for the pursuer's motion for a property transfer order in respect of the defender's share was made in the context of submissions which maintained that to achieve equal sharing of the value of the matrimonial property, a total transfer of value in excess of £90,000 required to be made by the defender to the pursuer. In that context, his submission was that that transfer should be effected partly by transferring the defender's share of the house to the pursuer, and partly by payment of a capital sum by the defender to the pursuer. Apart from her submission that any transfer of value should be from the pursuer to the defender, which I have rejected, counsel for the defender maintained that the pursuer had not led evidence to justify a property transfer order in respect of the defender's share of the house. Nothing had been said in evidence to make a case under s. 10(6)(d). Apart from the fact that there was evidence that the pursuer continued to live in the house, that is correct. But that would, in my view, have been nothing to the point if counsel for the pursuer had been correct in maintaining that a transfer of value of more than £72,500 required to be made by the defender to the pursuer in order to effect equal sharing of the net value of the matrimonial property. In the event, however, I have held that the pursuer holds matrimonial property to the value of £625,342, while the defender holds matrimonial property (net of the debts which he paid) to the value of £702,840. The difference is therefore £77,498, and the equalisation transfer of value would thus require to be approximately £38,750.11, therefore, the defender's share of the house were to be transferred, a balancing capital sum would require to be paid by the pursuer to the defender. For the reasons illustrated in *Wallis v. Wallis*, that is not, in my view, a very satisfactory way in which to adjust the matter. Given that the defender has offered an undertaking not to take any steps to realise his interest in the house until the parties' interests in P&B have been realised, I am of opinion that the best course is to make no property transfer order in respect of the house, but to make an award of a capital sum in the pursuer's favour payable once P&B has been sold. In that way, the pursuer will have the continued occupancy of the house until the capital which she has tied up in P&B is released, at which stage it will be for her to consider whether she wishes to buy out the defender's share of the house, or would prefer to concur in its sale, and purchase alternative accommodation. Correspondingly, the defender will not have to pay the capital sum until his tied up capital is released. Proceeding, therefore, in that way, I shall make an award of a capital sum of £38,750 in favour of the pursuer, but defer the defender's obligation to pay it until the capital tied up in P&B has been realised.

Sale of P&B

The pursuer's fourth conclusion is for an order for sale of both parties' shares in P&B and for an order that the whole free proceeds thereof under deduction of the expenses of sale and CGT be divided equally between the parties. In the end, however, counsel for the pursuer restricted his motion to one for an order for sale of the shares. The net proceeds of sale, after deduction of the costs of sale, would then fall to be divided in proportion to the parties' respective holdings, and each would bear CGT on the gain which he or she had realised. Counsel for the defender did not oppose the making of such an order, but submitted that the sale should be deferred for a period of three years. I shall return in due course to the question of the mechanics by which the sale ought to be carried into effect. It is necessary to consider first the competing submissions that the sale should be (i) immediate or (ii) deferred for three years.

Counsel for the defender advanced a number of reasons for deferring the sale. In the first place she pointed to the fact that, when the parties embarked through P&B on the hotel owning venture, it was intended that they should continue in it only for a limited period. The pursuer said in evidence that the intention was to continue for five years; the defender said five to six years. The company has traded for only about three and a half years. Part of the contemplated period therefore remains. Secondly, counsel argued that immediate sale made no commercial sense. Substantial funds had been ploughed into refurbishment of the hotel, but that was not yet reflected in an increase in turnover, and since the value of the business depended on turnover, the business required to continue in order to recoup what had been spent on refurbishment. There was support for that view in the evidence of Mr Gillies of Graham & Sibbald, Chartered Surveyors. He was an expert in the valuation of hotel businesses, and said at one stage in his evidence that the parties had little alternative to continuing with the redevelopment of the hotel. That would require further capital expenditure of the order of £40,000 to £50,000 to complete the renovation. His evidence was that it might take a further two years before the business would trade profitably, and that it might take up to 10 years before a sale price would be achieved which would recoup not only the original investment but also the additional money spent on refurbishment. Much would depend on the defender's management skill in the interim, and also to some extent on luck. Continuing to trade for 18 months to two years might achieve a better price although not recoupment of the investment. Counsel for the defender pointed to the evidence that the trading losses which have been suffered were in part attributable to dishonesty on the part of the employed management, at a time when the defender was not involved full time in management of the hotel. Insufficient time had so far passed since the defender took the management into his own hands full time to enable the benefits of that change to be seen in the profits. There was, however, potential for improvement if the hotel continued to trade. Thirdly, counsel submitted that the desirability of continuing to trade for a period before realising the asset was reinforced by consideration of the CGT implications. In that connection the pursuer had most to gain by delay. Two forms of relief were relevant: retirement relief, which was in process of being phased out, and taper relief, which was being phased in. The pursuer would not be entitled to retirement relief, but would benefit from taper relief. The defender would be entitled to either form of relief. Counsel for the defender submitted that from the defender's point of view the maximum tax advantage might be gained by delaying the sale for three or four years. Counsel also pointed out that the defender's ability to obtain alternative employment was limited by the restrictive covenant entered into in 1993, which was to subsist until 2000. The pursuer, on the other hand, had the benefit of pensions totalling about £6,000 per annum which she could, if she chose, draw now. She also had realisable capital at her disposal. She thus had sufficient means to tide her over until a sale of P&B in three years' time with, perhaps, some reduction in her lifestyle. In all the circumstances it was fair that the sale of P&B should be delayed for three years.

Counsel for the pursuer submitted that it was in neither party's interests that the sale should be delayed for any material period. From the point of view of CGT, early sale would enable the defender to make maximum use of his entitlement to retirement relief. If the business of P&B were carried on, there would be no prospect of a dividend, and therefore the pursuer would have no income from her capital tied up in the business. The defender, on the other hand, had said in evidence that he intended to draw a salary from the company. It was unfair to the pursuer to require her to continue to invest in the company with no return on her capital while depending on the management skills of the defender to improve the turnover and profitability of the company. To continue with the business was to take a risk with the remaining capital in the hope of future gain. It was one thing for the defender to do that with his own capital, but quite another for him to require the pursuer to submit to his doing it with hers.

In my opinion, the period of time for which the parties originally contemplated that they would continue to trade through P&B has, in the changed circumstances that now exist, very little bearing on whether the investment should be realised now or the realisation should be deferred. I accept that because of poor trading the value of the shareholding has fallen from the level at which it was at the relevant date. Mr Gilbert's evidence was that in the two years following the relevant date the aggregate value of the shares on a going concern basis fell from almost £900,000 to under £650,000 (no 28/1 of process, app 3). I accept the evidence that in part the poor performance was attributable to lax management at a time when the defender was still working for SOFEC and was therefore not maintaining full time supervision. No doubt some improvement will result from his personally taking control of the management of the hotel. He is, however, an amateur in hotel management, although he is no doubt experienced in business in a general sense. My impression from Mr Gillies' evidence was that there remained some reason for uncertainty as to whether the defender would bring sufficient skill to the direction of the hotel's affairs. The enterprise is, on Mr Gillies' evidence, too small to bear the cost of employment of full time professional management. The evidence is that, with successful management and completion of the refurbishment project, it will nevertheless take some considerable time before the value of the business can be built up sufficiently for a sale to recoup the original investment and the additional capital subsequently introduced (and in part still to be introduced) to fund the refurbishment. Mr Gillies' evidence was that that might take 10 years, although it might be achieved more quickly. The defender in evidence was more optimistic, but I prefer Mr Gillies' professional judgment. Improvement insufficient to recoup the entirety of the sums invested but sufficient to realise a better price than could be achieved at present will, no doubt, take place in a shorter period than 10 years, but I did not understand Mr Gillies to hold out any certainty of such improvement in a timescale as short as three years. So far as the impact of CGT is concerned, because the pursuer is not actively involved in the business and thus is not entitled to retirement relief, it would be to her benefit to wait for the impact of taper relief to increase. I would not, however, regard it as right to give weight to that consideration against the pursuer's expressed preference for immediate realisation. From the defender's point of view, delay progressively loses him the benefit of retirement relief, but correspondingly increases his entitlement to taper relief It is, however, impossible to know when, from the point of view of the defender's entitlement to relief from CGT, would be the most advantageous time to realise his shareholding, since what would be required for such a calculation would include knowledge of how the value of the business would move over time. To defer realisation of the shareholdings in P&B for three years would be to lock the pursuer in, for that period, to a business which in the meantime would offer her no return on her capital. I do not consider it appropriate to contrast with that lack of income to the pursuer the fact that the defender proposes to draw a salary from the company, provided that salary is set at a proper level to reflect the value of his management to the company rather than a return on his capital. But leaving that factor aside the difficulty about deferring sale for three years is that the pursuer is for that period deprived of the use of her capital. While there is a possibility of improvement in the value of the shares over a three year period, I do not consider that the evidence enables me to come to any clear conclusion as to their probable value at the end of that period, still less to work out what (if any) net gain after tax will probably be achieved. It is, in my view, significant that no attempt was made in counsel for the defender's submissions to quantify the benefits of delay. Where, as here, one party wishes immediate realisation and the other wishes a delay, one route to reconciliation of those aims is for one party to buy out the other. It was accepted, however, on both sides of the bar that that was not practicable in this case. I must therefore make a decision in favour of one or other of the proposed courses. In that situation I have come to the conclusion that the uncertainties about the future prospects of the business are such that there should be no deferral of the realisation.

That decision could be given effect by an immediate order under s. 14(1)(a) of the 1985 Act for sale of the parties' shares in P&B. The evidence, however, suggests that a better price may be obtained by selling the business owned by P&B as a going concern, then winding up P&B and distributing the funds thus realised between the parties in accordance with their respective shareholdings, rather than by a forced sale of the shares. Moreover, Mr Gillies suggested that the best price for the business might be achieved by selling it in a number of lots, separating in particular the chalets from the hotel. It seems to me that, now that the question of whether the realisation of the parties' investment in P&B should be deferred has been answered in the negative, the parties should have an opportunity to consider how best they should concur in effecting realisation of that investment.

Future Procedure

In the circumstances I propose, before pronouncing any decree, to put the case out by order for the purpose of hearing further submissions on how best to give effect to the decisions which I have made.

Unless either party identifies any difficulty which might arise in consequence of my doing so, I contemplate that I shall grant decree of divorce at the by order hearing.

I do not propose to make any property transfer order in respect of the contents of the matrimonial home. In calculating what order needs to be made to effect fair sharing of the matrimonial property, I have made the assumption that the defender will receive those items from the house that he expressed a wish to have, and that the pursuer will receive the remainder, without the need for any formal order to that effect.

As I have indicated, I am of opinion that the order for financial provision which is justified by the principles set out in s. 9 of the 1985 Act is one for payment by the defender to the pursuer of a capital sum of £38,750. Such an order in my opinion also satisfies the second requirement of s. 8(2). I consider, however, that it should take effect only once the defender's investment in P&B has being realised. The necessary postponement of the effect of the award of a capital sum might be achieved by making an order under s. 12(2), but I shall hear further submissions on that at the by order hearing.

If the defender does not renew his offer of an undertaking to refrain from realising his interest in the house until the investment in P&B has been realised, the point can be covered by an incidental order under s. 14(2)(d).

I contemplate that, if parties can agree on a procedure and timetable for marketing the business of P&B, I shall make no order for sale of the shares at this stage. If agreement proves impossible or breaks down, the possibility of such an order will remain. Procedurally there is no difficulty in achieving that, since a s. 14(1)(a) order may be made after the granting of decree of divorce. I shall hear submissions at the by order hearing as to the procedure for realisation which the parties wish to adopt.

Counsel for Pursuer, C.N. Macnair; Solicitors, Brodies, W.S.—Counsel for Defender, J.M. Scott; Solicitors, Morton Fraser.

R v. R

Outer House, December 7, 1999. Reported 2000 Fam.L.R. 43.

OPINION OF LORD EASSIE

Introductory
The parties to this action of divorce were married in Scotland on April 11, 1988. The pursuer comes originally from Finland but had lived in Scotland for some years prior to her marriage to the defender. She had previously been married and has a daughter—V, born June 19, 1984—by that marriage. When the defender married the pursuer he accepted V into family. The parties have three other children, namely H, born September 10, 1988, L, born October 11, 1991 and O who was born on March 10, 1996. The marital cohabitation endured for almost 10 years, the parties having separated on March 12, 1998 when the defender left the matrimonial home.

The defender does not oppose the granting of decree of divorce. Evidence in relation to the merits of the divorce was given by the pursuer and supporting evidence was provided, in affidavit form, by the pursuer's sister, Mrs C. Within that evidence there is sufficient to enable me to hold that the marriage has broken down irretrievably.

The parties are now agreed on the arrangements respecting the children. L and O are to reside with their mother, the pursuer, whereas H will stay with his father. Arrangements are in place whereby the three children are together each weekend, alternating between the homes of the pursuer and the defenders respectively. V attends boarding school and will continue to do so. During school holidays she stays principally with her mother but she also has contact with the defender.

In light of the evidence given by the parties and by the defender's aunt, Mrs I, I consider that the arrangements for the care and upbringing of the children are satisfactory. In these circumstances I shall grant decree of divorce and make a residence order to the effect that L and O reside with the pursuer and H with the defender. I shall make the order sought by the defender that he be given parental rights and responsibilities in respect of V, there being no opposition to such an order. Neither party seeks any further order in relation to V's residence or contact with her.

The remaining controversy between the parties concerns the financial provision to be made by the defender for the pursuer. Although agreement has been reached on the extent and value of the matrimonial property at the relevant date, the division of that property is in dispute, the principal issue being the contention on behalf of the defender that there exist special circumstances, particular special circumstances of the kind referred to in subsection (6)(b) of section 10 of the Family Law (Scotland) Act 1985—"the Act"—which justify a sharing of the matrimonial property on a basis other than equality and the primary contention for the pursuer that the property be divided equally.

The Net Value of the Matrimonial Property
Leaving aside the furniture and furnishings in the former matrimonial home which the parties have agreed to divide between them on an equitable basis, the total value of the matrimonial property has been agreed in the sum of £1,204,635. This agreement is contained in the joint minute, no. 19 of process.

The items forming the matrimonial property are inventoried in paragraph 1 of the joint minute as follows:

"a) B Farm valued at £292,000.
b) D House, valued at £415,000.
c) An account with the Dunfermline Building Society holding £650.
d) An NFU policy number 544505 valued at £6,840.
e) An NFU policy number 606089 valued at £1,470.
f) An Equitable Life Policy valued at £14,290.
g) An account with the Bank of Scotland account number 1970455 holding £272,196.
h) An account with the Bank of Scotland number 197181 holding £11,130.
i) An account with the Bank of Scotland account number 691783 holding £2,510.
j) An account with the Clydesdale Bank holding £400.
k) a PEP valued at £72,026.
l) A TESSA holding £11,048.
m) A business known as WB & AD R valued at £98,875.
n) Cow Quota valued at £1,200.

83

o) Three horses valued at £5,000".

With the exception of the last item on that inventory, all of the matrimonial property is owned by the defender. It appears that the three horses forming that last item were sold by the pursuer after the separation.

The Sources of the Net Matrimonial Property

It was not suggested in evidence that at the date of the marriage the pursuer had any significant capital assets. She had been employed as an assistant in a children's home in Perth and had previously done some work for a Swedish company. She was an accomplished horsewoman and was involved in show-jumping and consequently owned a horse or horses. By contrast, the defender was the owner of L Farm in Fife which had been gifted to him by his father some time prior to the marriage. The defender was also in partnership with his mother in the firm of W.B. & A.D. R. This was the family farming partnership. The partners at one time included the defender and both his parents but his father had retired some time prior to the date of the defender's marriage to the pursuer. In addition to carrying on farming at L the partnership also farmed the holding known as C Farm near Dunfermline. In 1988, when the parties married, C House and Farm was owned by the defender's father. However, by a disposition dated February 12, 1992 Mr R, Senior, donated C Farm to the defender (while retaining ownership of the mansion house and policies known as C House). In September 1993 the defender's mother died and in terms of her testamentary arrangements the defender succeeded to all of her interest in the partnership. The defender thereafter continued the farming business as a sole trader but used the name of the former family partnership as his trading style. Accordingly, by way of gift or inheritance the defender came to own both the farms of L and C and the whole of the farming business.

In the course of 1989 the defender sold part of L to Dunfermline District Council for use as a refuse coup. The consideration for the sale was some £30,000 in cash, which the defender banked initially and thereafter applied as additional capital in the farming business, and the conveyance (in part excambion) of an area of land adjacent to C Farm. In 1991 the defender was able to sell approximately 40 acres of L to a quarry company for use as a quarry. That sale attracted a price of £305,000. C Farm also turned out to have valuable minerals and the farm, together with the ground adjacent to it which had been obtained from the District Council, were sold in 1992 to an open cast coal mining company for a price of £751,000. The proceeds of this sale were also deposited in a bank account. The sale of C Farm was accompanied by an arrangement whereby the defender was given a tenancy of the farmhouse at C Farm and for some time after the sale the parties continued to live there.

The parties ceased to reside at C Farmhouse in about 1994 when the defender purchased at a price of £260,000 the house known as D House, Crieff, which became the parties' matrimonial home and remained so until the time of the separation. The purchase of D House was funded from the proceeds of the sales of farmland narrated above. Those sale proceeds also provided the source wherefrom the defender was able to purchase the farm of B, near Kinross, in 1995. Following the purchase of D, a considerable amount of money was spent on alterations to, and refurbishment and redecoration of, D House. No. 7/53 is a manuscript list prepared by the defender of the contractors' and tradesmen's bills incurred on those improvements. It was not disputed that the contractors' and tradesmen's charges were paid for by the defender, in large if not total measure from the funds realised by the sales of the farmland.

In addition to both the farms received by way of donation from his father and also his mother's interest in the partnership to which the defender succeeded by inheritance, the defender was the recipient of testamentary benefaction from other relatives. From the estate of Mrs Jessie R (the defender's step-grandmother) he received in 1991 shares with the value at that time of £17,487 (no. 7/50 of process). The estate of his grandmother, Mrs Margaret M, gave to the defender in 1991 shares then worth £5,219 (no. 7/52 of process). The defender gave evidence to the effect that his understanding was that, in accordance with advice given by his brother, a solicitor, those inherited shareholdings and others held by him prior to his marriage were rationalised in a personal equity plan—item (k)—to which additional annual payments had been made within the limits allowed under the personal equity plan legislation. Although the defender's brother did not give evidence and the precise details of the share transactions were not fully explored in evidence, I have no reason to reject the defender's understanding of that rationalisation and the subsequent additions to the PEP.

Among other matters canvassed in the defender's evidence were his bank accounts. The defender explained that the Bank of Scotland account which is item (g) on the inventory was the interest bearing account into which the proceeds of the sale of C and parts of L had been placed. The account listed at (h) on the inventory contained funds transferred from account (g), which was used to feed the Bank of Scotland account listed as (i). That account was the current account which the defender operated for ordinary day-to-day requirements. Since the farm business had always banked with the Clydesdale Bank he had also a personal account with that bank (item (j)).

So far as the insurance policies were concerned, the NFU policies had been set up some considerable time ago and the premia were paid by drawing on the "feeder" bank account. The Equitable Life Policy derived from a sale of a Hambro Life Policy which he had held since his youth.

In considering the extent to which the net value of the matrimonial property may have derived from gift or inheritance it is also, in my view, relevant to consider the evidence in relation to the parties' earnings during the marriage. Because the pursuer was performing the function of caring for the children and the household she was not in a position to make any significant financial contribution by way of actual earnings. It appeared that for a very brief period she and a cousin endeavoured to carry on a business of retailing dried flowers, but it was evidently not particularly profitable. So far as the defender's earnings are concerned, the accounts of the farming enterprise are to be found in nos. 7/4 and 7/52-61 of process. Those accounts are agreed accurately to show the profits and losses of the farming business. The accounts for the accounting year ending November 30, 1989 are missing but the figures for the defender's share of the net profit/(loss) and salary (prior to the mother's death) for the other years of the marriage are as follows:

1988	£5,521
1990	£12,204
1991	£6,065
1992	(£5,732)
1993	(£2,753)
1994	(£15,978)
1995	£12,949
1996	£8,831
1997	(£2,881)
1998	(£8,812)

For a limited period of time during the parties' cohabitation the defender had part-time employment with a firm of land agents and surveyors in Dunfermline, namely Macrae & Macrae. It appears that, anticipating the BSE crisis, the defender had sold-off most of the cattle on his farms and reduced the level of farming activity, he being, as he said, in the happy position of having substantial capital enabling him to ride out the BSE storm. In these circumstances he was able to take up employment with Macrae & Macrae. However, he did not find the office-based employment particularly congenial and he therefore reverted to farming on a full-time basis. At all events the total income received by the defender from his employment was modest—approximately £8,300 before tax.

In light of the evidence relating to the parties' earnings during the marriage and the largely undisputed evidence from the defender as to the sources and history of his patrimony, it is in my view plain that to a very large extent the net matrimonial property derives from the realisation of assets acquired by the defender by way of succession or gift and the interest accumulated on the deposited proceeds. It may be added that the defender retains ownership of L Farm (under exception of the parts sold off) but that does not constitute matrimonial property. I further add that neither counsel submitted that in addressing issues of the source of the agreed matrimonial property and its consequences for the fair sharing of that property any particular distinction should be drawn between the discrete items in the inventory contained in the joint minute. They accepted that a global approach should be adopted.

Equal Sharing

Section 9 of the Act enjoins the court, when deciding what order for financial provision should be made, to have regard to certain principles whereof principle (a) is that: "the net value of the matrimonial property should be shared fairly between the parties to the marriage".

Further provision in relation to the notion of "fair sharing" of the value of the matrimonial property is to be found in section 10 of the Act. Subsection (1) of section 10 provides: [His Lordship narrated the terms of the subsection and continued]

So far as concerns the term "special circumstances" employed in subsection (1) of section 10 further provision is made in subsection (6) of that section as follows: [His Lordship narrated the terms of subsection (6)(b) and (d) and continued]

Counsel for the pursuer—Mrs Davie—submitted that, notwithstanding the largely undisputed evidence that the bulk of the matrimonial property derived from assets gifted to the defender *inter vivos* or by testamentary provision, equal sharing should prevail. Under reference to *Little v. Little*, 1990 S.L.T. 785 and more particularly *Jacques v. Jacques,* 1997 S.C. (H.L.) 20 she submitted that there was effectively a presumption in favour of an equal division of the matrimonial property and that to overcome that presumption it was necessary that there be not just a special circumstance of the kind referred to in section 10(6) of the Act, but that the special circumstance or circumstances justified a departure from the presumption in favour of equality. The circumstance that much of the matrimonial property derived from inherited or gifted assets was not, she said, sufficient to justify a departure from the principle of equality. Counsel went on to submit—as I understood it—that where the inherited or donated assets had been used as a source wherefrom income was derived to provide the family with its means of support, the source of the capital funds ceased to be of relevance. Only if the inherited funds had been enclosed in a specific asset such as a "nest egg for retirement" would they be removed from the norm of equal division.

Mr Macnair for the defender submitted *inter alia* that the source of the matrimonial property in the present case constituted a special circumstance under section 10(6)(b) which clearly justified departure from the notion of equal division of the net value of the matrimonial property. Counsel referred to the underlying intention of the Act which he said was to achieve equal division of the wealth acquired during the marriage as a result of the efforts of the parties during its currency. Counsel referred to *Latter v. Latter*, 1990 S.L.T. 805; *Whittome v. Whittome*, 1994 S.L.T. 115 and The Scottish Law Commission Report. Very little of the accumulated capital worth in the net matrimonial property in the present case had been produced by the efforts of the parties, as opposed to inheritance or gift. Alongside such reported cases as *Davidson v. Davidson*, 1994 S.L.T. 506; *Adams v. Adams*, 1997 S.L.T. 144 and *McConnell v. McConnell (No. 2)*, 1997 Fam. L. R. 108 there was the unreported decision of the Lord Ordinary (Rodger) in *MacLean v. MacLean* (March 28, 1996), the facts of which were closer to the circumstances of the present case. A feature of *MacLean* was that by transacting with the inherited agricultural land, the owner (the wife pursuer) had been able to realise a special capital value in the land. The husband defender (the claimant spouse) had also worked on the farm, without remuneration, during the marriage. The Lord Ordinary departed from the presumption of equal sharing and had given the claimant defender but 25 per cent of the matrimonial property. Although, as counsel for the pursuer in the present case had pointed out, in *MacLean* it had been conceded that the origin of the matrimonial property constituted a special circumstance, that concession had been properly made by counsel for the wife pursuer in that case.

In my opinion the fact that to a large extent indeed the net value of the matrimonial property in this case derives from assets donated to or inherited by the defender does constitute a special circumstance which justifies departing from the presumption of an equal division of those assets. I consider that counsel for the defender is correct in saying that the broad policy underlying section 9(1)(a) and section 10 of the Act was that in principle an equal division should apply to the fruits of the economic efforts of the parties during the marriage. In his opinion in *Whittome*, Lord Osborne stated (at 126C):

"As I understand the policy of that part of the Act of 1985 which relates to the making of financial provision on divorce, which includes the fair sharing of 'matrimonial property', it is to the effect that, in general, the wealth acquired by the parties, subject to the statutory exclusion, or generated by their activity and efforts during the course of their life together is, in the absence of special circumstances, to be shared equally. The sharing exercise is not to be applicable to property acquired by one party or another by way of gift or succession from the third party".

That view is constant with the approach proposed by the Scottish Law Commission at paragraph 3.79 of its Report on Aliment and Financial Provision (Report No. 67):

"3.79 *Source of funds or assets.* Property bought after the marriage may have been paid for out of funds owned by one party at the time of the marriage. It may represent merely a switching of investments. We think that this should justify a departure from equal sharing. Similarly we think that a departure from equal sharing could be justified if the source of the funds or assets used by a spouse to acquire property during the marriage was a gift from a third party (such as a spouse's parent). The underlying principle is the sharing of property acquired by the spouses' efforts or income during the marriage. Property acquired wholly or partially with funds or assets derived from other sources need not be shared equally. The possible combinations of circumstances which might arise are such that, as noted above, we prefer to deal with this question by giving the court a discretion rather than by laying down any rule. In practice few couples own substantial assets at the time of marriage."

The same point is made in *Clive on Husband and Wife* at paragraph 24.031:

"CHANGES IN ASSETS. If non-matrimonial property (such as premarital property or a gift or legacy) is sold and the proceeds used during the marriage to acquire new property which is still owned at the relevant date, then the new property will be matrimonial property. However, the fact that the new property was acquired out of separate property is a special circumstance which could justify a departure from equal sharing. The reason for this approach is that it would have led to great complications to require the proceeds of separate property to be traced through various transactions. It was therefore deliberately decided to treat all property owned at separation and acquired by the spouses during the marriage(otherwise than by gift or inheritance) as matrimonial property, but to give the court a discretion to take account of the source of the funds used to acquire any particular item or part of it in deciding how it should be shared."

Mrs Davie's submission that the source of the funds ceased to be capable of being a special circumstance if the surrogate of the inherited or donated asset is used to provide income for the family is not supported or vouched by any of the authorities placed before me and in my opinion it runs counter to the evident intention or policy of the Act. In my view, when arriving at a fair division of the matrimonial property in this case, due weight must be given to the fact that to a very large extent it derives from inherited or gifted assets which, had they not been sold, would have been outwith the scope of matrimonial property.

The Other Principles

In addition to considering whether there are special circumstances justifying a departure from the presumption of equal sharing, it is necessary of course to consider the other principles to which one is required by the Act to have regard.

Section 9(1)(b) provides that: [His Lordship narrated the terms of the subsection and continued] For the purposes of applying that principle regard has to be had to the particular factors set out in section 11(2) of the Act.

It was said on behalf of the pursuer that the defender had received the economic advantage of having had the benefit of the pursuer's services as a housekeeper, nanny, hostess and assistant in the farm business, any salary paid to her from the farm being used in effect as her housekeeping money. The counterpart of that economic advantage conferred on the defender was that the pursuer had been economically disadvantaged by her being unable to pursue a career either by commercially applying her equestrian skills or by following a course in interior design which she had wished to do at one point in the marriage but to which it was alleged the defender had taken objection.

From the evidence led it was clear, and really not disputed, that the pursuer had done much as a housewife and a mother. Apart from the normal and demanding tasks required to be performed in the bringing up of the children, the pursuer had devoted energy into the decoration and improvement of C Farmhouse and later, particularly, in the organisation of the extensive refurbishment of D. There was some dispute in the evidence as to the extent to which the pursuer might physically have worked on the construction of the foundations of a conservatory which was added to the house at D but in my estimation that dispute is not of much materiality. My impression was that the pursuer was inclined to exaggerate the extent of her physical involvement. However that may be, I am satisfied that with her flair for interior design and decoration—readily conceded by the defender—and by her simply being present to supervise and deal with the tradesmen and contractors, the pursuer played an important practical role in facilitating the refurbishment of D, albeit that the tradesmen's bills were of course settled by the defender from his funds. It also appeared that, as might be expected, the pursuer assisted to a degree in some farm matters if need arose. She attended occasionally to such tasks as fetching spare parts for machinery, or collecting the carcasses of sheep slaughtered for family consumption, or assisting in the feeding of the beasts at weekends. However, that activity was in large measure incidental to her role as wife and mother.

In relation to the pursuer's career prospects had she not been married, as I have already narrated, prior to the marriage she was employed in a children's home in Perth. It was not, I think, suggested that this was a particularly well-paid employment with prospects for advancement to even better remuneration. The pursuer gave evidence that during the course of the marriage she had wished to take up study on an interior design course but that, despite her sister's willingness to fund the course, the defender had refused to allow her to pursue this potential career opportunity. In his evidence the defender said that he was unaware of the sister's willingness to pay for the course; he did not refuse to pay for it or allow her to follow it up; and essentially the pursuer lost interest in the idea.

I do not regard this area of dispute as being of any great import in the ultimate decision which

I have to take. However it is perhaps appropriate that I record my preference for the defender's version of events. My impression of the pursuer's evidence on this point was that, with hindsight, she was seeking to attach undue importance to the issue of the interior design course and the defender's supposed refusal to allow her to pursue it. I had the further impression that she believed that this might assist her financial claims in this action. However it appears to me to be on balance much more probable that in her busy life as a housewife, mother, organiser of tradesmen and the like, the pursuing of a course on interior design (which would have involved her being away from home) simply slipped down the daily agenda in terms of importance and eventually came to be dropped. At all events, as I have already mentioned, the defender readily acknowledged the pursuer's talent in matters of interior design. If she had not been married to the defender pursuing a career in interior design would have been an option alternative or additional to the commercial development of her interest in equestrianism.

In relation to the pursuer's interest in equestrian activities she deponed that she did have plans, or hopes, to set up a livery but after the marriage she was too busy with the upbringing of the children and other matters such as the refurbishment of D to pursue that activity on a commercial basis. Her hope was that, following divorce, she could acquire a suitable property in order to carry on business in training and coaching riders already engaged in competitive equestrian activity. Subject to her finding such a property, the pursuer appeared to have confidence that her equestrian talents and contacts would enable her to make a success of such a venture.

A further principle to which the court is directed to have regard is that enunciated in subsection (c) of section 9, namely: "Any economic burden of caring, after divorce, for a child of the marriage under the age of 16 years should be shared fairly between the parties". The various factors to which regard should be had in applying that principle are set forth in subsection 3 of section 11 but I do not think it necessary for me to rehearse them here.

At present the defender pays the school fees for V (whose father, I was given to understand, also makes an alimentary payment to the pursuer) and the defender pays aliment to the pursuer for L and O. He expressed his willingness to continue these arrangements. The defender has of course financial responsibility for H, who stays with him. It appeared to be accepted by counsel that should the defender not continue to honour his commitment to aliment the children in the pursuer's care—and I have no reason to believe that he will not keep his word—the Child Support Agency could then be brought into play and aliment secured in that fashion.

It thus appears that the economic burden of providing financially for the children will to a material extent remain with the defender but, that said, the pursuer will obviously require to address the capital need involved in acquiring a home suitable for the children in her care (and for H on his weekend visits to his mother and siblings) and that acquisition will in turn entail continued revenue expenditure on heating, maintenance and the like.

Counsel for the defender, for his part, pointed out that the defender, who currently stays with his widowed father, might wish to acquire his own home suitable for all the children to be together at weekends and that to some extent similar considerations would apply as regards the defender. However, in his evidence the defender did not suggest that in the immediate or relatively near future he had under contemplation moving from C House.

Neither counsel suggested that the principle contained in subsection (e) of section 9(1) of the Act had any pertinence in the present case but counsel for the pursuer sought to invoke section 9(1)(d) in the event that the court were not to accede to her motion that the pursuer be awarded one-half of the net matrimonial property. She submitted that in order to continue to have a comfortable lifestyle the pursuer required that one-half share. On investing capital in a house with land and other facilities appropriate to enable the pursuer to develop her equestrian business she would only have the balance available to provide an income. (This assertion prima facie seemed to ignore the point that the equestrian business would in time provide an income but I assumed it to advert to a transitional stage.) For his part counsel for the defender resisted the suggestion that there be an award of periodical allowance. He pointed to the restriction on the award of periodical allowance effected by the Inner House in *McConnell (No. 2)* and adverted to the terms of section 13 of the Act, particularly subsection (2) thereof.

Discussion

As I have already stated, I am entirely satisfied that special circumstances exist justifying a departure from the presumption of equal sharing of the matrimonial property and that I require to give appropriate weight to the factor that the great bulk of the matrimonial property stems from assets which were inherited by or given to the defender.

As regards the other principles to which I must have regard I can, I think, summarise my views by saying that I consider that the pursuer has suffered some financial disadvantage by being unable to pursue an independent economic activity because of her natural commitment to the care of the children and the organisation of the family home, including in particular the design-input and *de facto* superintendence of the refurbishment of D. While it is no doubt true, as counsel for the defender stated in the course of his submissions, that there was no evidence showing that an equestrian establishment such as the pursuer had in mind would have been readily profitable, I do not think it necessary that detailed accountancy evidence of such matters be presented in proceedings such as these. One in effect recognises the inability of the wife to follow up an independent economic activity because of her maternal and marital responsibilities. On the other hand, and among other matters, the pursuer's talent for interior design and her availability to superintend and deal with tradesmen in the refurbishment of D constitutes to my mind a material advantage to the defender both in its direct consequences for the property at D and his ability otherwise to pursue his farming activities.

In considering the pursuer's economic disadvantage I must also take into account the fact that had the marriage not occurred her ability to pursue an independent economic activity would be subject to any limitation stemming from her the requirement to provide suitable arrangements for the care of V.

In relation to the future financial burden of caring for the children under the age of 16 I recognise the defender's willingness to continue to pay aliment for the children. However, I also perceive that the simple payment of aliment is not the whole story and that the provision by the pursuer of suitable accommodation for the children presents additional but not readily quantifiable costs and to that extent at least some of the burden of caring for the children must necessarily fall upon her.

As regards Mrs Davie's submission that, in the absence of an equal division of the matrimonial property a periodical allowance should be awarded I have to say that given the limited (if any) profits derived by the defender from his farms, it appears to me that any award of periodical allowance would require to be paid out of his capital. I therefore consider that the appropriate way to proceed is by assessing a suitable capital payment (*cf.* section 13(2)(b) of the Act).

I would also record that whereas counsel for the pursuer contended for an award to her client of 50 per cent of the matrimonial property, Mr Macnair for the defender submitted—under particular reference to the Lord Ordinary's decision in *MacLean*—that 25 per cent of that matrimonial property was "the top of the range" and that the appropriate figure should lie between £250,000 and £300,000.

While the Act provides guidance on the approach to be taken by the court in determining the amount of financial provision, it is important to appreciate that at the end of the day the matter is one for the exercise of a judicial discretion. As it was put by the Lord President Hope in *Little* v. *Little*, in a passage approved in the House of Lords in *Jacques*, "... the matter is essentially one of discretion, aimed at achieving a fair and practicable result in accordance with common-sense".

While appreciating the force of Mr Macnair's submissions that the special circumstances of the origin of the matrimonial property require a departure from the presumptive norm of equal sharing, I take the view that his approach did not give sufficient weight to the pursuer's position as respects the other principles, especially principle (b) [economic advantages/disadvantages]. In the whole circumstances, exercising the essentially discretionary judgment which I have to apply and endeavouring to achieve a fair and practicable result, I have come to the view that a fair sharing of the matrimonial property will be achieved by my awarding to the pursuer a capital sum of £380,000.

Since it was indicated to me that an award of a capital sum of that amount might involve questions as to a deferment of the date of payment of a proportion thereof, pending sale of D, I shall, as requested, put the case out by order for discussion on the timetable for payment of that capital sum and the interest, of any, payable thereon.

Counsel for Pursuer, Davie; Solicitors, Drummond Miller, W.S.—Counsel for Defender, Macnair; Solicitors, Balfour & Manson, W.S.

INDEX

References are to sections and Schedules

AGREEMENTS ON FINANCIAL PROVISION, 7, 16
  setting aside, 16
  varying, 16
ALIMENT
  adopted children, 1
  actions for, 2
    allowable circumstances, 2
    and Child Support Act, 2
    expenses of, 22
    powers of court, 3
    small amounts, 23
    supporting information, 3
  agreements, 7
  amount, 4
    factors considered, 4
  backdating, 3, 5
  calculation of, 4
  changes in circumstance, 5
  and Child Support Agency, 4
  children, 1, 2
    adopted, 1
    educational expenses, 3
    foster, 1
    further education, 1, 2
    training, 1
  claims, 2, 3
  deceased's estate, 1
  decree of, 2, 3
    variation or recall, 5
  and earning capacity, 4
  foster children, 1
  income calculation, 4
  interim, 6
  interim variation, 5
  married couples, 1
  material facts
    non-disclosure, 5
  needs taken into account, 4
  persons owing obligation, 1
  parents, 1, 2
  periodical payments, 3
  reasonable, 1
  and refusal of divorce or separation, 21
  separation, 2
  short term arrangements, 6
  unmarried couples, 1
AMENDMENTS, 28
ANNULMENTS, 17
ARRESTMENT, 19
AVOIDANCE TRANSACTIONS, 18

BUSINESS INTERESTS, 10, 11

CAPITAL GAINS TAX, 10

CAPITAL PAYMENT ORDER, 8, 9, 12
  instalments, 12, 13
  method, 12
  pension lump sums, 12A
  and periodical allowance, 13
  timing, 12
CAREER CONSIDERATIONS, 11
CHILD SUPPORT AGENCY
  and negotiated contracts for aliment, 4
CHILDREN
  parents' obligation to aliment, 1, 2
  adopted, 1
  foster, 1
  further education, 1, 2
  training, 1
CITATION, 29
COMMENCEMENT, 29
CONSEQUENTIAL AMENDMENTS, Sched. 1

EARMARKING ORDER, 12A

DEBTS
  and financial provision order, 10
  and matrimonial property, 10

EARNING CAPACITY, 11
EDUCATION
  children
    expenses, 3
    further, 1, 2
  retraining on divorce, 11
EXPENSES OF ACTIONS, 22
EXTENT, 29

FINANCIAL INFORMATION PROVISION, 20
FINANCIAL PROVISION ORDERS, 8
  and age, 11
  and business interests, 11
  career disadvantaged, 11
  and debts, 10
  and duration of dependence, 11
  and earning capacity, 11
  economic advantage or disadvantage, 9, 11
  and financial prudence, 11
  and health, 11
  matrimonial home
    increase in value, 11
    non-financial contribution to, 11
  matrimonial property see Matrimonial property
  and other financial obligations, 11
  principles applied in calculating, 9, 11

91

FINANCIAL PROVISION ORDERS—*cont.*
and secured loan payments, 11
special circumstances, 10

HARDSHIP, 9
HEALTH, 11
HOUSEHOLD GOODS, 25
HOUSEKEEPING ALLOWANCE, 26

INCIDENTAL ORDERS, 14
INHIBITION, 19
INSURANCE POLICIES, 14
INTEREST, 14
INTERPRETATION, 27

LEGAL CAPACITY AND MARRIAGE, 24
LIFE POLICIES, 10
LOAN PAYMENTS, 11

MATRIMONIAL HOME, 10, 14
increase in value, 11
local authority discount, 10
non-financial contribution to, 11
MATRIMONIAL PROPERTY, 10
alienation of property, 10
business interests, 10
and capital gains tax, 10
contents valuation, 10
damages, 10
date of cessation of cohabitation, 10
and debts, 10
destruction of property, 10
dissipation of property, 10
and financial obligations, 11
and financial prudence, 11
increase in value, 10, 11
life policies, 10
local authority discount, 10
matrimonial home, 10, 11
net value, 10
no matrimonial property, 11
non-financial contribution to matrimonial
home, 11
non-matrimonial funds, 10
pensions, 10, 12A
redundancy payments, 10
relevant date, 10
secured loan payments, 11
share options, 10
sharing value, 10

MATRIMONIAL PROPERTY—*cont.*
sources of funds, 10
special circumstances affecting division, 10
and tax due, 10
third party rights, 15
unequal sharing, 10, 11
MOTION AND SPECIFICATION PROCEDURE, 14, 20

NULLITY OF MARRIAGE, 17

PENSIONS, 8, 10
earmarking order, 12A
lump sums, 12A
pension sharing, 12A
PERIODICAL ALLOWANCE, 9, 11
backdating, 13
and capital payments, 13
and changes of circumstance, 13
and cohabitation, 11
limited, 11
orders, 13
refused, 11
specific period, 11
suspended awards, 13
unlimited, 11
PROPERTY RIGHTS AND MARRIAGE, 24
PROPERTY SALE *see* Sale of property
PROPERTY TRANSFER ORDER, 8, 9, 12
and heritable creditors, 8
method, 12
timing, 12
PROPERTY VALUATION ORDER, 14

REDUNDANCY PAYMENTS, 10
REPEALS, 28, Sched.2
RESOURCES
provision of details, 20

SALE OF PROPERTY, 8
increase in value, 8
order, 14
SAVINGS, 28
SEPARATION
agreement *see* Agreements on financial provision
and aliment, 2
SHARE OPTIONS, 10

TAX DUE, 10
UNMARRIED COUPLES, 1